AF254853

# Shadow Work Journal and Workbook

*A Complete Guided System for Releasing Emotional Blockages, Working Through Past Experiences, Deepening Self-Awareness, and Reclaiming Your Authentic Power*

# Your Free Gift
# (only available for a limited time)

Thanks for getting this book! If you want to learn more about various spirituality topics, then join Mari Silva's community and get a free guided meditation MP3 for awakening your third eye. This guided meditation mp3 is designed to open and strengthen ones third eye so you can experience a higher state of consciousness. Simply visit the link below the image to get started.

https://spiritualityspot.com/meditation

Or, Scan the QR code!

*Shadow Work Journal and Workbook: A Complete Guided System for Releasing Emotional Blockages, Working Through Past Experiences, Deepening Self-Awareness, and Reclaiming Your Authentic Power*

**Review by Carolina Estevez, Psy.D., Licensed Psychologist**

As a psychologist, I approach shadow work resources with a balance of openness and clinical discernment, and *Shadow Work Journal and Workbook: A Complete Guided System for Releasing Emotional Blockages, Working Through Past Experiences, Deepening Self-Awareness, and Reclaiming Your Authentic Power* stands out as a thoughtfully structured and accessible guide for deep self-exploration. This book successfully bridges reflective insight with practical application, making it useful both for individuals engaging in personal growth and for clinicians seeking tools to support their therapeutic work.

Part 1, the Shadow Work Journal, is especially effective in guiding readers through the emotional arc of inner work. The Introduction establishes a compassionate and nonjudgmental tone that helps readers feel safe entering vulnerable emotional territory. Section 1, Confrontation, invites honest self-examination and encourages readers to face disowned or avoided aspects of themselves without shame. Section 2, Acceptance, skillfully reframes emotional wounds as meaningful experiences rather than deficits, reinforcing self-compassion and emotional validation—key components of psychological healing.

Section 3, Release, provides a sense of empowerment by helping readers identify and let go of limiting beliefs and emotional blockages that often maintain maladaptive patterns. Section 4, Integration, is one of the book's strongest elements, emphasizing wholeness rather than suppression, which aligns well with contemporary therapeutic models that value parts-based integration. Section 5, Authenticity, thoughtfully connects internal healing to external living, encouraging readers to embody their insights in daily life. The conclusion offers grounding and reinforces that shadow work is an ongoing, evolving process.

Part 2, the Shadow Work Workbook, complements the journal by translating insight into action. The workbook introduction clearly prepares readers for active engagement. Chapters on understanding the shadow, meeting it directly, and recognizing triggers, patterns, and projections are presented in a clear, approachable manner without oversimplifying complex psychological concepts. The focus on daily routines in Chapter 5 is particularly valuable, as it helps sustain change through consistent, manageable practices. The bonus 369 Shadow Worksheets provide ample opportunities for repetition, reinforcement, and personalization of the work.

Overall, *Shadow Work Journal and Workbook: A Complete Guided System for Releasing Emotional Blockages, Working Through Past Experiences, Deepening Self-Awareness, and Reclaiming Your Authentic Power* offers a comprehensive, well-organized system for shadow work that respects emotional depth while remaining accessible. It encourages self-awareness, emotional integration, and authenticity in a way that is empowering and inspirational.

# Table of Contents

# Part 1: Shadow Work Journal

*Guided Prompts and Questions to Integrate Your Shadow, Release Emotional Blockages, and Express Your Authentic Self*

# Introduction

No one is perfect. Everyone has an Achilles heel, makes mistakes, and suffers from emotional scars. All of these are part of being human. You can't go through life without negative emotions, unpleasant thoughts, or socially unacceptable desires. You deny these aspects of yourself, keeping them hidden, afraid of being judged or rejected for who you really are.

Denying certain aspects of your personality can damage your mental health, emotional health, and well-being. You need to accept and embrace every part of yourself. This can be done with shadow work.

Shadow work basically involves connecting with your unconscious mind to reveal your repressed personality so you can heal and fully accept yourself.

This book introduces the concept of the "Shadow Self" and the importance of acknowledging the hidden parts of yourself. It will help you come to terms with your darkness, accept yourself, and find emotional freedom.

Your darker side is the result of your trauma and pain. Your unhealed emotional wounds tend to eventually create a barrier when it comes to forgiving yourself and your past.

Most limiting beliefs can restrict your freedom and keep you from growing, meeting your goals, or realizing your true potential. This is why overcoming these thoughts and emotions will set you up to be who you have dreamed of being. You will be able to face your fears and self-doubt once you find what triggers them.

You can't truly recognize your strength if you've never acknowledged your weaknesses, just as you can't fully appreciate your light without having encountered darkness. Each person is a mix of highs and lows, filled with both defeats and victories. You can't just focus on one side and ignore the other; embracing all parts of your personality is essential for finding inner peace.

The final section of the book guides you in accepting your true self by aligning your actions and behaviors with your core values and beliefs. It encourages you to conquer your fears and break free from societal expectations, allowing you to lead a meaningful life without the weight of judgment or rejection. Plus, each chapter includes thoughtful journal prompts designed to help you reflect and gain a deeper understanding of yourself.

**The Benefits of Reading Shadow Work Journal Book:**

- Gaining a deeper understanding of shadow work and how it can bring awareness to repressed emotions and hidden beliefs

- Clarity in identifying emotional wounds and negative thought patterns

- A safe space to explore and release repressed emotions through guided prompts and creative expression

- The ability to integrate the shadow self and heal past trauma

- The creation of a consistent, mindful practice for personal growth

# Section 1: CONFRONTATION

# Face Your Shadow Self

Coming to terms with some of the more unsightly elements of your personality – like anger, sadness, or cruelty – is a challenge many people face. Most individuals choose to ignore these aspects of themselves and bury them deep within. The shadow self cannot be denied indefinitely. Concealed feelings, perceptions, and opinions will eventually manifest through crying or uncontrolled rage. To heal and grow, acceptance of these repressed aspects is the only way forward.

Identifying and facing your shadow self is the first step to healing.[1]

The purpose of this chapter is to describe your shadow self, enabling you to explore your hidden emotions, beliefs, and past memories with a set of prompts and questions.

# What Is the Shadow Self?

Certain aspects of one's personality, including fears, emotions, and desires, are referred to as the *shadow self.* It is the version of yourself that you struggle to accept and is in deep slumber, so to speak. The majority of people suppress the traits that embarrass them or simply do not conform to societal expectations. A reflection of someone's shadow self is usually buried underneath. Acceptance and recognition of this aspect requires reflection and thoroughly comprehending your character.

The term "The Shadow" was first used by Swiss psychologist Carl Jung, who attributes it to the savage parts of an individual. In Jung's words, each individual possesses dual sides, including the persona that everyone can see, or in other words, one's public personality, and the shadow self, the concealed, sinister half that resides within.

Rather than perceiving the shadow self as a sinister side, Jung considered it a neutral component of a person that must be examined to attain a better grasp of one's self. To some degree, he claimed that it is impossible to uncover the shadow side without first understanding the persona. That is when a person can seize their irrational urges.

Suppressing your shadow self can have troubling consequences. You might experience a lack of self-worth, anxiety, depression, a holier-than-thou attitude, narcissism, self-defeat, difficulty forming relationships, being misleading, and harmful and aggressive behavior.

Your shadow self is extremely vital to understand because it is the most sensitive part of your personality. Particular circumstances can be motivational, or it can go the other way around – you might project self-doubt and blame your shortcomings on others. For instance, if you suppress sadness, you might look down on people who mourn openly or even go to the extreme of disciplining children for crying.

Never avoid or feel shame when it comes to your shadow self. It is something that calls for nurturing and healing. Accepting all dimensions of your personality can enable true emotional freedom, self-respect, and wholeness.

Shadow work allows you to tap into your unconscious to reveal and confront traumatic or undesirable patterns of your personality. It involves journaling, self-reflection, visualization, and other techniques to awaken self-awareness and self-acceptance.

Once you begin shadow work, you will start seeing your shadow self in a different light and learn to treat it with love and compassion.

**Benefits of Shadow Work**

- Boosting self-esteem
- Improving creativity
- Self-awareness
- Self-compassion
- Self-acceptance
- Feeling sympathetic towards other people's shadow selves
- Improving well-being

# Prompts and Questions

This journaling section helps start the process of facing the shadow self. However, this is only the beginning of your journey.

**Emotions that Feel "Too Much"**

Reflect on your hidden or suppressed emotions, such as sadness, shame, or anger.

1. What emotions do you struggle with facing or expressing?

_________________________________________________

_________________________________________________

_________________________________________________

_________________________________________________

_________________________________________________

_________________________________________________

_________________________________________________

2. Why can't you acknowledge and confront these emotions?

_________________________________________________

_________________________________________________

_________________________________________________

_________________________________________________

_________________________________________________

_________________________________________________

_________________________________________________

3. What do these emotions need from you?

_______________________________________________
_______________________________________________
_______________________________________________
_______________________________________________
_______________________________________________
_______________________________________________
_______________________________________________

4. What do you usually feel when you experience overwhelming emotions?

_______________________________________________
_______________________________________________
_______________________________________________
_______________________________________________
_______________________________________________
_______________________________________________
_______________________________________________

5. When do you usually feel powerless and unable to control your emotions?

_______________________________________________
_______________________________________________
_______________________________________________
_______________________________________________
_______________________________________________
_______________________________________________

6. What emotions do you usually judge others for or project on them?

_______________________________________________
_______________________________________________
_______________________________________________
_______________________________________________
_______________________________________________
_______________________________________________

7. What parts of yourself do you keep from your loved ones?

 

8. What emotions are you embarrassed to express to your loved ones?

 

9. What makes you feel defensive? What parts of yourself are you trying to protect?

 

10. What do you physically feel when you are scared or anxious?

 

11. What overwhelming emotions do you hide in social situations?

12. How are you feeling right now?

13. What is the most dominant emotion you feel now? How do you feel it in your body?

14. What triggered this emotion?

15. Do you have unresolved conflicts that affect your emotions? How do you deal with them?

16. What parts of yourself do you reject?

17. What parts of yourself do you judge harshly?

18. What emotions have you been carrying for so long, and do you need to release them?

19. What is the one emotion you wish you could share with others but are afraid of being judged?

________________________________________________

________________________________________________

________________________________________________

________________________________________________

________________________________________________

________________________________________________

________________________________________________

20. Do you act angry, but underneath, you feel a different emotion? What is this emotion?

________________________________________________

________________________________________________

________________________________________________

________________________________________________

________________________________________________

________________________________________________

________________________________________________

21. Do you feel that you have to hide certain emotions to be accepted?

________________________________________________

________________________________________________

________________________________________________

________________________________________________

________________________________________________

________________________________________________

________________________________________________

22. Pick the emotions that resonate with you.


## PICK THE EMOTIONS
## THAT RESONATE WITH YOU


- ☐ Fear
- ☐ Sadness
- ☐ Shame
- ☐ Anger
- ☐ Fear
- ☐ Guilt
- ☐ Emptiness
- ☐ Jealousy
- ☐ Frustration
- ☐ Loneliness
- ☐ Helplessness
- ☐ Inadequacy
- ☐ Anxiety
- ☐ Depression
- ☐ Failure
- ☐ Resentment

**Past Experiences**

Consider moments when you have felt rejected, judged, or misunderstood. This helps bring hidden wounds to the surface for exploration.

1. Think of a time when you felt rejected or unloved. How did you react to that experience, and how do you feel about it now?

____________________________________________

____________________________________________

____________________________________________

____________________________________________

____________________________________________

____________________________________________

2. Have you ever felt that you wanted to be someone else so people would love you?

____________________________________________

____________________________________________

____________________________________________

____________________________________________

____________________________________________

____________________________________________

3. Is there a moment you wish you could have said something, but you held back your words out of fear of being misunderstood or judged?

____________________________________________

____________________________________________

____________________________________________

____________________________________________

____________________________________________

____________________________________________

4. What past experience brings back feelings of anger, pain, or rejection?

_______________________________________________
_______________________________________________
_______________________________________________
_______________________________________________
_______________________________________________
_______________________________________________
_______________________________________________

5. When was the last time you were hard on yourself? What made you feel that way?

_______________________________________________
_______________________________________________
_______________________________________________
_______________________________________________
_______________________________________________
_______________________________________________
_______________________________________________

6. When was the last time you felt misunderstood? What prompted this emotion?

_______________________________________________
_______________________________________________
_______________________________________________
_______________________________________________
_______________________________________________
_______________________________________________
_______________________________________________

7. When was the last time you were embarrassed of your emotions? Why did you feel that way?

_______________________________________________
_______________________________________________
_______________________________________________
_______________________________________________
_______________________________________________
_______________________________________________

8. Have you ever manipulated others to hide your vulnerability or out of fear that people won't accept you?

9. Why do you think that people won't love or accept your shadow self?

10. Are you struggling with feeling unloved? What people or situations made you feel that way?

11. Do you want to confront the people who rejected you? What would you tell them?

12. What major life event made you feel judged, rejected, or misunderstood?

________________________________________

________________________________________

________________________________________

________________________________________

________________________________________

________________________________________

________________________________________

13. Are you purposely making people misunderstand you to hide aspects of your personality?

________________________________________

________________________________________

________________________________________

________________________________________

________________________________________

________________________________________

________________________________________

14. Has a loved one ever judged or rejected you? How did that make you feel? What do you wish you could tell them now?

________________________________________

________________________________________

________________________________________

________________________________________

________________________________________

15. When was the last time someone misunderstood you? How did it make you feel?

________________________________________

________________________________________

________________________________________

________________________________________

________________________________________

16. When was the last time you felt unloved? How did that make you feel?

_______________________________________________

_______________________________________________

_______________________________________________

_______________________________________________

_______________________________________________

_______________________________________________

17. What or who triggers feelings of rejection?

_______________________________________________

_______________________________________________

_______________________________________________

_______________________________________________

_______________________________________________

_______________________________________________

**My Shadow Self-Profile**

Imagine your shadow self as a real person and answer these questions.

1. What does your shadow self currently look like?

_______________________________________________

_______________________________________________

_______________________________________________

_______________________________________________

_______________________________________________

2. How does it act?

_______________________________________________

_______________________________________________

_______________________________________________

_______________________________________________

_______________________________________________

_______________________________________________

3. How does it react?

4. What triggers your shadow self?

5. What are the dominant traits of your shadow self?

6. Is your shadow self angry for being hidden? What does it want to say?

7. How does it react to criticism?

__________________________________________________

__________________________________________________

__________________________________________________

__________________________________________________

__________________________________________________

__________________________________________________

8. When was the last time you prevented your shadow self from expressing its emotions? How did that make it feel? What did it want to say?

__________________________________________________

__________________________________________________

__________________________________________________

__________________________________________________

__________________________________________________

__________________________________________________

9. Imagine hugging your shadow self and treating it with compassion. How does it feel now?

__________________________________________________

__________________________________________________

__________________________________________________

__________________________________________________

__________________________________________________

__________________________________________________

10. Draw what your shadow self looks like now.

11. Write a letter to your shadow self.

_______________________________________________
_______________________________________________
_______________________________________________
_______________________________________________
_______________________________________________
_______________________________________________
_______________________________________________
_______________________________________________
_______________________________________________
_______________________________________________
_______________________________________________
_______________________________________________
_______________________________________________
_______________________________________________
_______________________________________________
_______________________________________________
_______________________________________________
_______________________________________________
_______________________________________________

Your shadow self is a part of you. It represents your mistakes, anger, fears, and embarrassing moments. These aspects make you human. You can't avoid them all your life. Embrace your shadow self and accept it. It is hurt and broken, so treat it with love and compassion.

# Section 2: ACCEPTANCE

# Embrace Your Inner Wound

Your shadow self is shaped by emotional trauma, pain, and scars you carry with you. These are elements of your life you wish not to bring to the surface, and despite your efforts to stay away from them, you only risk feeling compromised. Accepting your wounds will enable you to feel whole.

Embracing your wounds will allow you to overcome them.[2]

This chapter addresses the approach to healing trauma by confronting emotional wounds. More importantly, it encourages you to take care of the parts that feel broken by providing stepping stones to identify and nurture the pain.

# The Importance of Accepting Your Emotional Wounds

Acknowledging your emotional wounds is paramount to achieving integration and wholeness. The healing process requires you to embrace your emotional wounds and change your relationship with your pain, so what was an experience of suffering can ultimately be your greatest strength. You should not look at your past with regret. You must learn from it and get on with living your life. Emotional wounds are simply part of life. You cannot avoid emotional pain in your life. You must lose loved ones, miss out on hopes and dreams, and endure difficulties. Just as meaningful times are part of life, painful times are a noteworthy part of life. You must experience both sides of life to live it fully. When you try to live a life free from emotional pain, you will never feel whole. You will always feel like a piece of you is missing. Emotional wounds are part of your being. They are part of your lived experiences, and they are part of your life lessons. Accepting the brutality of life means you wholeheartedly accept all of yourself and all the life you have lived.

Most emotional wounds originate from early experiences, relationships, and social conditioning. For instance, if you loved someone and had a bad breakup, you may experience emotional pain each time you think of them. Abusive parents also leave emotional scars that time may not heal.

Many people struggle to move on from their past. They believe that healing requires forgetting the painful experiences or those who hurt them. Emotional healing is about forgiving yourself or others while carrying the lessons you have learned. Instead of holding on to the pain and letting it consume you, you transform it into compassion and wisdom. You allow your past to make you a better person, free of anger and regrets.

## Benefits of Embracing Emotional Wounds

- Improve your physical health

- Increase resilience

- Boost your emotional intelligence

- Enhance mental health

- Reduce the risk of mental illness

- Increase productivity

- Healthy relationships

- Encouraging personal growth

## Vulnerability and Self-Compassion

According to researcher Brené Brown, embracing your vulnerability can make you more resilient and help you lead an authentic life. She urges people to be kinder and more understanding towards themselves and practice self-compassion during tough times to overcome challenges.

Many people are afraid of showing their vulnerable side. However, Brown explains that vulnerability is a gift, not a weakness. Only courageous and confident individuals can share this part of themselves.

Being vulnerable involves sharing your deepest thoughts and feelings without fear of judgment or rejection. When you show people your most authentic self, you create a safe space for them to be vulnerable as well. This allows you to build strong relationships based on mutual trust.

Vulnerability allows you to unlock your full potential to become the person you have always wanted and achieve your goals. You will stop being afraid of failure, treat every mistake as a learning opportunity, and accept your strengths and weaknesses.

Brown also states that you can overcome negative emotions with self-compassion. When you are sad or have self-doubt, imagine someone you love is going through the same experience. Talk to yourself as if you are talking to them. Be kind, positive, and supportive.

## Childhood Trauma

According to psychologist and philosopher Alice Miller, childhood trauma can have a huge impact on a person's life. The first three years of a child's life are crucial in their brain development. Traumatized children can become more stressed or violent.

**If you've experienced trauma in your childhood, this is something you need to confront.**[3]

Growing up with abusive parents who emotionally neglected and never validated or supported you can be traumatic. The emotional scars toxic parents leave can negatively impact every aspect of your life.

Don't let your past pain impact your future. Acknowledge your inner child's needs and give yourself the support and validation your parents didn't give you. Reclaim your emotional freedom and understand and accept your past to overcome its influence. When you heal your inner wounds, you give yourself the freedom to be happy and confident and build healthy relationships.

Healing from past wounds doesn't mean forgetting the pain. You are simply not letting it define you or ruin your present and future.

# Prompts and Questions

The prompts and questions in this section will help you identify your emotional wounds, understand where they originated from, and begin the healing process with self-compassion.

### Emotional Wounds From the Past

Identify the wounds you have carried all your life.

1. What are the deepest emotional wounds you carry?

2. How have these wounds shaped the way you view yourself and others?

3. Describe your childhood.

4. Were your parents warm and loving or cold and distant? How has their behavior affected you?

_______________________________________________

_______________________________________________

_______________________________________________

_______________________________________________

_______________________________________________

_______________________________________________

_______________________________________________

_______________________________________________

5. What do you feel when you think about your childhood?

_______________________________________________

_______________________________________________

_______________________________________________

_______________________________________________

_______________________________________________

_______________________________________________

_______________________________________________

_______________________________________________

6. How have your emotional wounds impacted your life and relationships?

_______________________________________________

_______________________________________________

_______________________________________________

_______________________________________________

_______________________________________________

_______________________________________________

_______________________________________________

_______________________________________________

7. Is there a past experience that makes you angry? Why?

_______________________________________________

_______________________________________________

_______________________________________________

_______________________________________________

_______________________________________________

_______________________________________________

_______________________________________________

8. Do you wish you could get closure from a certain person? What do you want them to tell you?

_______________________________________________

_______________________________________________

_______________________________________________

_______________________________________________

_______________________________________________

_______________________________________________

_______________________________________________

_______________________________________________

9. Do you blame yourself for your emotional wounds? Why?

_______________________________________________

_______________________________________________

_______________________________________________

_______________________________________________

_______________________________________________

_______________________________________________

_______________________________________________

_______________________________________________

10. How does your inner child feel now?

_______________________________________________

_______________________________________________

_______________________________________________

_______________________________________________

_______________________________________________

_______________________________________________

_______________________________________________

11. What can you do to make it feel better?

_______________________________________________

_______________________________________________

_______________________________________________

_______________________________________________

_______________________________________________

_______________________________________________

_______________________________________________

_______________________________________________

12. What do you see when you look in the mirror?

_______________________________________________

_______________________________________________

_______________________________________________

_______________________________________________

_______________________________________________

_______________________________________________

_______________________________________________

_______________________________________________

13. Do you struggle with trusting others? Why?

14. How do your emotional wounds affect your mental and physical health?

15. What do you feel when you think about your emotional wounds?

16. If you could go back in time, what advice would you give your past self to protect them from these wounds?

____________________________________________

____________________________________________

____________________________________________

____________________________________________

____________________________________________

____________________________________________

____________________________________________

____________________________________________

## Shame and Self-Criticism

Reflect on how shame might be affecting your healing.

1. In what areas of your life do you carry feelings of shame or self-blame?

____________________________________________

____________________________________________

____________________________________________

____________________________________________

____________________________________________

____________________________________________

____________________________________________

____________________________________________

2. How can you begin to release these feelings and practice self-compassion?

____________________________________________

____________________________________________

____________________________________________

____________________________________________

____________________________________________

____________________________________________

____________________________________________

____________________________________________

3. Is there something in your life you blame yourself on? What is it?

4. How does shame affect your life?

5. Do you blame yourself for every bad thing that happens to you? Why?

6. What does your inner critic often tell you?

_______________________________________________

_______________________________________________

_______________________________________________

_______________________________________________

_______________________________________________

_______________________________________________

_______________________________________________

_______________________________________________

7. How do you silence this voice?

_______________________________________________

_______________________________________________

_______________________________________________

_______________________________________________

_______________________________________________

_______________________________________________

_______________________________________________

_______________________________________________

8. Do you judge yourself harshly? Why? What do you often say to yourself?

_______________________________________________

_______________________________________________

_______________________________________________

_______________________________________________

_______________________________________________

_______________________________________________

_______________________________________________

_______________________________________________

9. Do you use criticism to motivate yourself? Do you believe there are better ways to motivate yourself?

10. Does your shame or inner critic affect your healing? How?

11. When was the last time you criticized yourself? Write down the words you used.

12. How do shame and self-blame affect your life?

_______________________________________________

_______________________________________________

_______________________________________________

_______________________________________________

_______________________________________________

_______________________________________________

_______________________________________________

_______________________________________________

13. Write a letter to the part of yourself that feels shame.

_______________________________________________

_______________________________________________

_______________________________________________

_______________________________________________

_______________________________________________

_______________________________________________

_______________________________________________

_______________________________________________

_______________________________________________

_______________________________________________

_______________________________________________

_______________________________________________

_______________________________________________

_______________________________________________

_______________________________________________

_______________________________________________

_______________________________________________

_______________________________________________

_______________________________________________

14. Draw what shame feels like.

## Forgiveness and Letting Go

Healing often requires forgiveness, both of others and yourself. Reflect on who or what you need to forgive to move forward.

1. Who do you need to forgive, including yourself, to truly heal?

_____________________________________________________________________________________________________________________________________________________________________________

2. How can you begin the process of letting go of past hurt?

_____________________________________________________________________________________________________________________________________________________________________________

3. What is the one mistake you can't forgive yourself for? How can you release it and move on?

_____________________________________________________________________________________________________________________________________________________________________________

4. Reflect on a time when someone forgave you. How did that make you feel?

5. How do grudges affect your life? What can you do to move towards forgiveness?

6. What can you do today to practice empathy and forgive someone who has hurt you?

7. What can you let go of to be at peace?

8. What negative thoughts and beliefs are preventing you from forgiving yourself and others?

9. Write a letter of forgiveness to someone who has hurt you.

10. Write a letter of forgiveness to yourself.

## The Impact of Past Trauma

Reflect on how past trauma has affected your life and answer these questions.

1. How has past trauma influenced your thoughts, behaviors, and relationships?

2. What steps can you take today to begin healing these old wounds?

3. How has your traumatic experience influenced your decisions?

4. How has your trauma affected your loved ones?

5. Imagine you have healed from your trauma. How does that make you feel?

6. What does healing feel like?

7. How can you control your life and prevent your past from influencing your present?

8. How would your life be different if you didn't experience that traumatic event?

_______________________________________________

_______________________________________________

_______________________________________________

_______________________________________________

_______________________________________________

_______________________________________________

_______________________________________________

_______________________________________________

9. Write a letter to the person responsible for your trauma.

_______________________________________________

_______________________________________________

_______________________________________________

_______________________________________________

_______________________________________________

_______________________________________________

_______________________________________________

_______________________________________________

_______________________________________________

_______________________________________________

_______________________________________________

_______________________________________________

_______________________________________________

_______________________________________________

_______________________________________________

_______________________________________________

_______________________________________________

10. Draw your past self and your future/desired self next to it.

Don't let your past wounds influence your present and future. Accept them, forgive yourself and others, and move on with your life.

# Section 3: RELEASE

# Cast Away Limiting Beliefs and Emotional Blockages

Have you ever caught yourself thinking you just aren't cut out for something—maybe because you believed you lacked the strength or smarts needed? Life tends to toss around those nagging ideas that keep you stuck. You end up doubting your talents, constantly questioning what you're capable of, and before you know it, you're trapped by these negative voices. Generally speaking, if you let that inner critic lead, you risk missing out on real rewards and end up with more regrets than wins.

Limiting beliefs hold you back from moving forward.'

In this chapter, we take a closer look at those limiting beliefs and their quiet yet steady hold on your everyday experiences. It shows you, in a pretty down-to-earth way, how to flip the script on those discouraging thoughts and, in most cases, clear out the emotional clutter that's been blocking your progress.

# Limiting Beliefs

Limiting beliefs are the negative thoughts and assumptions you hold about yourself, others, or the world. In life, they drag you down, denying you access to your true potential. This pattern of thoughts usually develops at an early age from early experiences that shape us, the way we are brought up, failures that we have experienced, societal norms, or negative self-talk.

For example, a child with neglectful and emotionally detached parents may internalize the belief that they are unlovable. A girl growing up in a male-dominated society will think that she can't ever accomplish what she wants or go far in life.

Your decisions, your self-image, how you view things, and your interpretation of situations are all affected by limiting beliefs. They keep you from making leaps or seizing opportunities. Imagine your boss assigns you and other employees work and will promote whoever has the best idea. If you think that you aren't bright enough or will never be promoted, you will not put your best effort into the assignment, and this will obviously keep you from being promoted. The person who gets promoted may, in fact, not have the skill set or talent you possess, but they have believed in themselves and played the game.

You may also experience these thoughts about others. You may believe that all people are bad or that all marriages end in divorce. As a result, you will end up depriving yourself of genuine friendships or committed relationships.

Limiting beliefs can be a defense mechanism to protect you from pain. Let's say you had a negative experience in a few job interviews. You may stop going to new ones to protect yourself from disappointment or rejection.

These thoughts and perceptions lower your self-esteem and your motivation, keeping you stuck in patterns of fear or self-doubt.

Limiting beliefs aren't as powerful as you may think. While they can impact your life, they are nothing more than thought patterns that can be changed with reframing techniques.

Releasing limiting beliefs doesn't mean forgetting your past experiences. You are simply restructuring these thoughts to liberate yourself from their restricting hold.

# Cognitive Reframing

Cognitive reframing is a technique that shifts your mindset and changes how you feel about a person, relationship, or situation. It focuses on your thought pattern to transform the negativity into positivity. Say you believe that you will never get promoted at work. You keep saying, "I am not good enough," or "I don't have the skills to advance in my career." You can use cognitive reframing and imagine yourself as a lawyer trying to find proof to contradict these thoughts. What evidence supports that you aren't good at your job? If you are a bad employee, why didn't they let you go? You will eventually realize that these thoughts have no basis.

Psychologist Dr. Aaron Beck developed the cognitive reframing technique in the 1960s to help patients suffering from depression think positively. He believed that your interpretation of a situation, not the situation itself, entices a reaction from you. For instance, a person may be upset when it rains because it prevents them from going out and seeing their friends. Others will see it as an opportunity to stay at home and play games or watch a movie with their family.

Your thoughts and actions don't define you. They represent your reaction to an event. You can control them if you change how you look and approach any situation.

# Emotional Blockages

Emotional blockages keep you from feeling or expressing your emotions. Oftentimes, you don't understand how you feel or why you are experiencing a certain emotion. It is a defense mechanism that prevents you from accepting your emotions, thinking clearly, and reacting properly to a situation.

Emotional blockages usually occur when you avoid your emotions. When you ignore your feelings, they overpower you, leaving you angry, easily triggered, and confused. This can impact your relationships, mental health, career, social life, behavior, and cognitive skills. They can also hinder your personal growth, leaving you stagnant.

Releasing these blockages involves identifying their root causes.

### Causes of Emotional Blockages

- Past experiences
- Societal conditioning
- Inner self-critic
- Negative thoughts
- Fear and anxiety
- Stress
- Traumatic experiences
- Serious diseases
- Surprising lifestyle changes
- Losing a job
- Breakup or divorce
- Death of a loved one

Psychologist and psychotherapist Dr. Peter Levine created a type of alternative therapy called "Somatic Experiencing" to help people suffering from trauma. He believed that trauma is stored in the body, causing mental, physical, and emotional issues.

Traumatic experiences can cause disconnection from one's body. Somatic experiencing involves using specific techniques that can bring awareness to your emotions, physical sensations, and internal experiences.

# Prompts and Questions

The prompts and questions in this section will help you identify your limiting beliefs, explore their origins, and reframe them into empowering perspectives.

### My Limiting Beliefs

Explore the beliefs that hold you back and change how you see yourself, your life, other people, experiences, etc., that are often buried beneath the surface.

1. What beliefs about yourself do you rarely share with others? When did you first start believing this about yourself?

_______________________________________________

_______________________________________________

_______________________________________________

_______________________________________________

_______________________________________________

_______________________________________________

_______________________________________________

_______________________________________________

2. How did past experiences or external influences shape this belief?

_______________________________________________

_______________________________________________

_______________________________________________

_______________________________________________

_______________________________________________

_______________________________________________

_______________________________________________

_______________________________________________

3. What beliefs are holding you back from achieving your goals or living the life you want?

_______________________________________________

_______________________________________________

_______________________________________________

_______________________________________________

_______________________________________________

_______________________________________________

_______________________________________________

_______________________________________________

4. Write down three limiting beliefs that affect your relationships.

_______________________________________________

_______________________________________________

_______________________________________________

_______________________________________________

_______________________________________________

_______________________________________________

_______________________________________________

5. Write down three limiting beliefs that prevent you from advancing in your career.

_______________________________________________

_______________________________________________

_______________________________________________

_______________________________________________

_______________________________________________

_______________________________________________

_______________________________________________

_______________________________________________

6. Write down three limiting beliefs that affect your social life.

_______________________________________________

_______________________________________________

_______________________________________________

_______________________________________________

_______________________________________________

_______________________________________________

_______________________________________________

_______________________________________________

7. Write down three limiting beliefs you have about yourself.

8. Write down three limiting beliefs you have about your family.

9. Write down three limiting beliefs you have about your friends.

10. Write down three limiting beliefs you have about people in general.

_______________________________________________________

_______________________________________________________

_______________________________________________________

_______________________________________________________

_______________________________________________________

_______________________________________________________

_______________________________________________________

_______________________________________________________

11. Write down three limiting beliefs you have about life.

_______________________________________________________

_______________________________________________________

_______________________________________________________

_______________________________________________________

_______________________________________________________

_______________________________________________________

_______________________________________________________

_______________________________________________________

12. Reflect on your childhood; what limiting beliefs prevented you from achieving your goals? Where did they stem from?

_______________________________________________________

_______________________________________________________

_______________________________________________________

_______________________________________________________

_______________________________________________________

_______________________________________________________

_______________________________________________________

_______________________________________________________

13. When you think of limiting beliefs, do you hear your voice or your parent's or teacher's voice telling you that you aren't good enough?

14. Why do you give these beliefs so much power?

15. Are these your beliefs, or has someone influenced you, like society, friends, parents, etc.?

16. Are these beliefs helping you grow? How do they make your life better?

_______________________________________________

_______________________________________________

_______________________________________________

_______________________________________________

_______________________________________________

_______________________________________________

_______________________________________________

_______________________________________________

17. Write down three opportunities you have missed or goals you couldn't achieve because of these beliefs.

_______________________________________________

_______________________________________________

_______________________________________________

_______________________________________________

_______________________________________________

_______________________________________________

_______________________________________________

_______________________________________________

_______________________________________________

18. What can you do now to achieve these goals?

_______________________________________________

_______________________________________________

_______________________________________________

_______________________________________________

_______________________________________________

_______________________________________________

_______________________________________________

_______________________________________________

_______________________________________________

19. What do your limiting beliefs protect you from?

20. Will you be happier if you let go of your limiting beliefs? Why?

21. How do your limiting beliefs affect your daily life?

22. What has your inner critic been telling you lately?

_______________________________________________

_______________________________________________

_______________________________________________

_______________________________________________

_______________________________________________

_______________________________________________

_______________________________________________

_______________________________________________

23. Do you believe your limiting beliefs have positive intentions? What are they?

_______________________________________________

_______________________________________________

_______________________________________________

_______________________________________________

_______________________________________________

_______________________________________________

_______________________________________________

_______________________________________________

24. When you think of your story, what words do you use to describe yourself and your life?

_______________________________________________

_______________________________________________

_______________________________________________

_______________________________________________

_______________________________________________

_______________________________________________

_______________________________________________

_______________________________________________

25. Write a farewell letter to one of your most powerful limiting beliefs. Thank it for its internet and express how it has influenced your life. Explain that it's time now to move on from it to another belief that will help you on the next part of your journey.

## Reframing Limiting Beliefs

Challenge and reframe your limiting beliefs into more positive and empowering thoughts.

1. Write one limiting belief.

2. Acknowledge that it is a limiting belief, not a fact.

_______________________________________________

_______________________________________________

_______________________________________________

_______________________________________________

_______________________________________________

_______________________________________________

_______________________________________________

_______________________________________________

3. How does this limiting belief make you feel?

_______________________________________________

_______________________________________________

_______________________________________________

_______________________________________________

_______________________________________________

_______________________________________________

_______________________________________________

_______________________________________________

4. How does it impact your life?

_______________________________________________

_______________________________________________

_______________________________________________

_______________________________________________

_______________________________________________

_______________________________________________

_______________________________________________

_______________________________________________

5. Where does this belief stem from?

6. Is this belief true? Write down why you think it is or isn't true.

7. If you believe it is true, you can question it. Write down three or four questions and their answers to prove whether it is based on facts or negative thoughts.

8. Imagine letting go of this belief. How does that make you feel?

_______________________________________________

_______________________________________________

_______________________________________________

_______________________________________________

_______________________________________________

_______________________________________________

_______________________________________________

_______________________________________________

9. How will you challenge future limiting beliefs?

_______________________________________________

_______________________________________________

_______________________________________________

_______________________________________________

_______________________________________________

_______________________________________________

_______________________________________________

_______________________________________________

10. How does it feel to replace limiting beliefs with positive thoughts?

_______________________________________________

_______________________________________________

_______________________________________________

_______________________________________________

_______________________________________________

_______________________________________________

_______________________________________________

_______________________________________________

11. What small steps can you take to move away from these beliefs?

12. Mention some of your most empowering beliefs.

13. Imagine a life without your limiting beliefs. What does this version of you believe in and feel?

14. How can these beliefs serve you now?

______________________________________________
______________________________________________
______________________________________________
______________________________________________
______________________________________________
______________________________________________
______________________________________________
______________________________________________

15. Describe a perfect day without these limiting beliefs.

______________________________________________
______________________________________________
______________________________________________
______________________________________________
______________________________________________
______________________________________________
______________________________________________
______________________________________________

16. What would you be doing right now if your limiting beliefs didn't exist?

______________________________________________
______________________________________________
______________________________________________
______________________________________________
______________________________________________
______________________________________________
______________________________________________
______________________________________________

17. Think of some of your limiting beliefs. Rephrase them to become more positive and empowering.

18. What would you do now if these positive and empowering statements were true?

19. How can you use these positive beliefs instead of the old ones?

20. How can you learn from your mistakes instead of allowing them to reinforce your limiting beliefs?

21. What makes you get up in the morning?

22. What if your limiting beliefs were true? What is the worst that could happen?

23. How can you save yourself from this worst-case scenario? Write down in detail what you will do if something bad happens. (This will show you that even if one limiting belief is true, you can always salvage the situation, removing the power of this belief.)

## Reframing With Affirmations of Empowerment

Affirmations are short and positive statements that can change your thought pattern, helping you adopt a more confident mindset. You should repeat them every day multiple times to overpower your negative beliefs.

1. Write down five affirmations that you will repeat each time you experience this limiting belief.

2. How can you remind yourself daily of your worth and potential?

3. What positive words do you use to describe yourself and your achievements?

______________________________________________________________

______________________________________________________________

______________________________________________________________

______________________________________________________________

______________________________________________________________

______________________________________________________________

______________________________________________________________

______________________________________________________________

4. Write three things about your life for which you are grateful.

______________________________________________________________

______________________________________________________________

______________________________________________________________

______________________________________________________________

______________________________________________________________

______________________________________________________________

______________________________________________________________

______________________________________________________________

5. What makes you the most proud of yourself?

______________________________________________________________

______________________________________________________________

______________________________________________________________

______________________________________________________________

______________________________________________________________

______________________________________________________________

______________________________________________________________

______________________________________________________________

## Affirmations

- I am letting go of my limiting beliefs
- I can overcome challenges
- I question my negative beliefs
- I am smart and successful
- My mistakes don't define me
- I am in control of my thoughts
- I deserve to be happy
- I have what it takes to achieve my goals
- I seize every opportunity that comes my way
- I make a positive impact on people's lives
- I have people in my life who love me and want the best for me
- I am grateful for my life
- I am enough
- I love myself
- I trust my skills and abilities
- I am where I am supposed to be

## Confronting Emotional Blockages

Reflect on unresolved emotions that might be holding them back.

1. What emotions have you been suppressing or avoiding?

_______________________________________________

_______________________________________________

_______________________________________________

_______________________________________________

_______________________________________________

_______________________________________________

_______________________________________________

_______________________________________________

_______________________________________________

2. How can you create a safe space to process and release these feelings?

________________________________________________

________________________________________________

________________________________________________

________________________________________________

________________________________________________

________________________________________________

________________________________________________

________________________________________________

3. Are you distracting yourself from your true feelings? How?

________________________________________________

________________________________________________

________________________________________________

________________________________________________

________________________________________________

________________________________________________

________________________________________________

________________________________________________

4. Do you struggle with communicating your feelings? If yes, why?

________________________________________________

________________________________________________

________________________________________________

________________________________________________

________________________________________________

________________________________________________

________________________________________________

________________________________________________

5. What emotions do you struggle with expressing the most? Why?

6. How different would your life be if you could express your emotions?

7. How do you feel right now?

8. When was the last time you felt happy and safe?

______________________________________________

______________________________________________

______________________________________________

______________________________________________

______________________________________________

______________________________________________

9. When was the last time you cried? Did you cry in front of others or alone?

______________________________________________

______________________________________________

______________________________________________

______________________________________________

______________________________________________

______________________________________________

10. Write a "letter of release" to yourself or someone connected to the blocked emotion, expressing everything you have been holding in. You can then destroy the letter as a symbolic act of letting go.

______________________________________________

______________________________________________

______________________________________________

______________________________________________

______________________________________________

______________________________________________

______________________________________________

______________________________________________

______________________________________________

______________________________________________

______________________________________________

______________________________________________

______________________________________________

**Breaking Free from Fear**

Address the fears that prevent you from changing and growing.

1. What fears keep you stuck in old patterns?

2. What would it feel like to move past these fears?

3. How are your fears preventing you from changing and growing?

4. What would your life be like if your fears didn't control you?

5. Where do these fears stem from?

6. When was the last time your fear prevented you from achieving a goal?

_______________________________________________

_______________________________________________

_______________________________________________

_______________________________________________

_______________________________________________

7. What is your biggest fear?

_______________________________________________

_______________________________________________

_______________________________________________

_______________________________________________

_______________________________________________

8. Is this fear real or the result of negative thoughts, your upbringing, or society's influence?

_______________________________________________

_______________________________________________

_______________________________________________

_______________________________________________

_______________________________________________

9. How can you overcome this fear?

_______________________________________________

_______________________________________________

_______________________________________________

_______________________________________________

_______________________________________________

10. Describe how it would feel to be free from your fears.

_______________________________________________

_______________________________________________

_______________________________________________

_______________________________________________

_______________________________________________

11. What do your fears tell you each time you try to change or get out of your comfort zone?

_______________________________________________

_______________________________________________

_______________________________________________

_______________________________________________

_______________________________________________

### Releasing Through the Body

Emotional blockages are connected to physical tension. Your suppressed emotions can give you headaches and make you tired.

1. Where in your body do you feel tension or discomfort when you think about your blockages?

_______________________________________________

_______________________________________________

_______________________________________________

_______________________________________________

_______________________________________________

2. What can you do to release this energy?

_______________________________________________

_______________________________________________

_______________________________________________

_______________________________________________

_______________________________________________

3. How do you feel when you release this energy?

_______________________________________________

_______________________________________________

_______________________________________________

_______________________________________________

_______________________________________________

4. What emotions manifest physically?

_____________________________________________

_____________________________________________

_____________________________________________

_____________________________________________

_____________________________________________

5. Does each emotion have a different sensation?

_____________________________________________

_____________________________________________

_____________________________________________

_____________________________________________

_____________________________________________

6. Have you tried talking about your emotions when they manifested physically? How did that make you feel?

_____________________________________________

_____________________________________________

_____________________________________________

_____________________________________________

_____________________________________________

Limiting beliefs aren't facts. They are negative thoughts manipulating you to make you question your abilities. Reframe the negativity with positivity and focus on what you can do instead of what you can't do.

# Section 4: INTEGRATION

# Merge with All Parts of You

Every part of you deserves to be loved. You need to embrace your darkness and weakness to appreciate your light and strength. Personal growth requires self-acceptance and respecting all different aspects of your personality.

Embrace your darkness and weaknesses to find your strength for self-love.[5]

This chapter explains the concept of integration and individualism. You will also find various prompts to help you find balance between your light and shadow, embrace your imperfection, and find self-acceptance.

# Self-Integration

Self-integration is creating a balanced relationship with all aspects of your personality. It involves acknowledging your neglected parts and integrating your positive and negative sides.

You can't live a fulfilling life if you hide one part of yourself. Integrating your light and darkness is essential to make you whole. Self-integration is a crucial part of shadow work. It harmonizes your behavior, values, actions, thoughts, and emotions to make you feel complete. This allows you to thrive in every aspect of your life without suppressing or denying your authentic self. When you are at peace with every aspect of yourself, everything in your life works smoothly.

Self-integration leads to self-love, self-awareness, self-acceptance, clarity, and a deeper understanding of the self. It involves observing your different experiences, emotions, and thoughts without judgment. You acknowledge and engage with every aspect of your personality, even the frustrating ones.

When you are self-integrated, all aspects of your personality are unified. You love every part of you, allowing you to thrive and live happily.

Self-integration is different from perfection. It is about finding peace and accepting all parts of yourself without rejecting your mistakes or trying to be perfect.

Disintegration, on the other hand, causes imbalance since every part of you is competing with the other instead of working together.

## Principles of Self-Integration

- Taking responsibility for your decisions, actions, and mistakes.
- Living in alignment with your needs and values.
- Embracing your authentic self no matter how challenging life gets.
- Understanding that every aspect of your personality makes you whole, even the parts that contradict each other. You should accept and listen to each one of them.

Benefits of Integration

- Mental stability
- Peace of mind
- Lack of mental health issues like depression and anxiety
- Decision-making skills
- Maintaining healthy relationships
- Clarity
- Having purpose
- High self-esteem
- Consistent behavior
- Ability to resist external influences
- Reduced stress and exhaustion
- High productivity
- Spiritual connection

# Carl Jung's Concept of Individuation

According to Carl Jung, individuation is when a person becomes an individual, separate from the whole. It involves recognizing your unique characteristics and becoming your own authentic self. This allows you to accept your consciousness and the unconscious. The purpose of individuation is to develop your personality and let go of the false persona you use in public.

Jung created this concept from personal experience. He had a mid-life crisis that drove him to confront different aspects of his personality; Jung spent years trying to understand himself and become a better person.

Individuation takes you on a journey to understand yourself better. It allows you to become the most integrated version of your unique self and integrates the unconscious parts of the self into conscious awareness. It reveals who you are underneath the mask you wear to hide your negative side. You answer the question of who you would be if you made peace with your deepest secrets, darkest desires, and biggest mistakes.

The individuation process happens naturally. You don't choose to walk this path; life pushes you to it to learn, change, and grow.

# Dr. Kristin Neff's Work on Self-Compassion

According to Dr. Kristin Neff, self-compassion is showing kindness and compassion to oneself. You treat yourself with love and understanding instead of listening to your inner critic every time you make a mistake or fail. You become your biggest cheerleader and support yourself during hard times instead of being judgemental or feeling defeated in the face of adversity.

Self-compassion can be a coping mechanism in tough situations and helps you become more resilient. It improves your physical and mental health and encourages you to make changes, grow, achieve your goals, and do everything in your power to be happy.

# Prompts and Questions

The prompts and questions in this section help you explore the integration of your light and dark sides. They invite you to reflect on your imperfections, acknowledge your past wounds, and integrate all aspects of your personality to start healing.

### Balancing Light and Shadow

Reflect on the parts of yourself you have rejected or suppressed to achieve a more balanced understanding of your identity.

1. What aspects of your personality are you struggling to acknowledge?

2. How can accepting these parts make you whole?

3. Do you have a dark side that scares you?

_______________________________________________

_______________________________________________

_______________________________________________

_______________________________________________

4. What parts of yourself have you rejected, and how can you start accepting them?

_______________________________________________

_______________________________________________

_______________________________________________

_______________________________________________

5. What parts of yourself are you proud of, and which ones are you trying to avoid?

_______________________________________________

_______________________________________________

_______________________________________________

_______________________________________________

_______________________________________________

6. Do you feel that your light and dark side are competing or getting along?

_______________________________________________

_______________________________________________

_______________________________________________

_______________________________________________

_______________________________________________

7. Imagine your dark and light sides as people. What do they look like?

_______________________________________________

_______________________________________________

_______________________________________________

_______________________________________________

_______________________________________________

8. What are their most dominant characteristics?

9. What can you do to integrate them?

10. Describe your light side in five words.

11. Describe your shadow side in five words.

12. Imagine your light side writing a letter to your shadow side to make it feel loved and accepted. What would it say?

13. Create two drawings that represent contrasting aspects of yourself. One can represent your "light" self (positive traits, strengths, or joyful moments), and the other can represent your "shadow" self (hidden fears, doubts, or perceived weaknesses).

**Embracing Imperfection**

Integration involves accepting your imperfections. You need to self-reflect on your flaws and love every part of you.

1. How has striving for perfection hindered your personal growth?

2. How might embracing your imperfections support your journey toward self-acceptance?

3. What high standards do you constantly hold yourself to?

4. Which of these high standards do you find unrealistic?

5. Is your perfection holding you back?

6. Why are you afraid of embracing your mistakes and flaws?

_______________________________________________
_______________________________________________
_______________________________________________
_______________________________________________
_______________________________________________

7. How do you feel when you think of embracing your imperfections?

_______________________________________________
_______________________________________________
_______________________________________________
_______________________________________________
_______________________________________________

8. What would your life be like if you accepted your imperfections?

_______________________________________________
_______________________________________________
_______________________________________________
_______________________________________________
_______________________________________________

9. How do you feel when you make a mistake or when something isn't perfect?

_______________________________________________
_______________________________________________
_______________________________________________
_______________________________________________
_______________________________________________

10. What would you tell a friend struggling with embracing imperfections?

_______________________________________________
_______________________________________________
_______________________________________________
_______________________________________________

11. How does your fear of imperfections hold you back in life?

_______________________________________________
_______________________________________________
_______________________________________________
_______________________________________________
_______________________________________________

12. Do you struggle with accepting your imperfections out of fear of judgment?

_______________________________________________
_______________________________________________
_______________________________________________
_______________________________________________
_______________________________________________

13. How can you forgive your imperfections?

_______________________________________________
_______________________________________________
_______________________________________________
_______________________________________________
_______________________________________________

14. What is your fear of imperfection protecting you from?

_______________________________________________
_______________________________________________
_______________________________________________
_______________________________________________
_______________________________________________

15. What do you think will happen if you make a mistake?

_______________________________________________
_______________________________________________
_______________________________________________
_______________________________________________
_______________________________________________

16. How would your life change if people saw your imperfections?

_______________________________________________

_______________________________________________

_______________________________________________

_______________________________________________

_______________________________________________

17. What parts of your life would improve if you embraced your imperfections?

_______________________________________________

_______________________________________________

_______________________________________________

_______________________________________________

_______________________________________________

18. Why do your imperfections scare you?

_______________________________________________

_______________________________________________

_______________________________________________

_______________________________________________

_______________________________________________

19. Does your family, society, or environment influence your fear of imperfection? In what way?

_______________________________________________

_______________________________________________

_______________________________________________

_______________________________________________

_______________________________________________

20. What would happen if you, your work, or your life were imperfect?

_______________________________________________

_______________________________________________

_______________________________________________

_______________________________________________

_______________________________________________

## Gratitude for Imperfection Journaling

Every day, write down moments where you embrace imperfection, like leaving your hair messy, making a mistake, or not meeting your usual standards, and choose to practice self-compassion instead.

_______________________________________________
_______________________________________________
_______________________________________________
_______________________________________________
_______________________________________________
_______________________________________________
_______________________________________________
_______________________________________________
_______________________________________________
_______________________________________________
_______________________________________________
_______________________________________________
_______________________________________________
_______________________________________________
_______________________________________________
_______________________________________________
_______________________________________________
_______________________________________________

## Compassionate Self-Acceptance

Self-compassion is a way to foster integration. Always be kind and compassionate to yourself.

1. How do you treat yourself when you make a mistake?

_______________________________________________
_______________________________________________
_______________________________________________
_______________________________________________
_______________________________________________

2. What would it look like if you treated yourself with the same compassion you offered others?

_______________________________________________

_______________________________________________

_______________________________________________

_______________________________________________

_______________________________________________

3. What do you like about yourself?

_______________________________________________

_______________________________________________

_______________________________________________

_______________________________________________

_______________________________________________

4. What don't you like about yourself? Is it worth changing?

_______________________________________________

_______________________________________________

_______________________________________________

_______________________________________________

_______________________________________________

5. If you can change it, how can you improve yourself?

_______________________________________________

_______________________________________________

_______________________________________________

_______________________________________________

_______________________________________________

6. If you can't change it, how can you make peace with it?

_______________________________________________

_______________________________________________

_______________________________________________

_______________________________________________

_______________________________________________

7. How do you respect yourself?

_______________________________________________

_______________________________________________

_______________________________________________

_______________________________________________

_______________________________________________

8. Do you hold yourself to unrealistic high standards?

_______________________________________________

_______________________________________________

_______________________________________________

_______________________________________________

_______________________________________________

9. How do you practice self-care every day?

_______________________________________________

_______________________________________________

_______________________________________________

_______________________________________________

_______________________________________________

10. Write five things you love about yourself.

_______________________________________________

_______________________________________________

_______________________________________________

_______________________________________________

_______________________________________________

11. When was the last time you practiced self-compassion? What did you tell yourself?

_______________________________________________

_______________________________________________

_______________________________________________

_______________________________________________

_______________________________________________

12. Imagine you failed at something; what would you tell yourself to feel better?

_______________________________________________

_______________________________________________

_______________________________________________

_______________________________________________

_______________________________________________

13. How do you silence your inner self-critic?

_______________________________________________

_______________________________________________

_______________________________________________

_______________________________________________

_______________________________________________

14. How can you support yourself better?

_______________________________________________

_______________________________________________

_______________________________________________

_______________________________________________

_______________________________________________

15. Write down ten things you are grateful for.

_______________________________________________

_______________________________________________

_______________________________________________

_______________________________________________

_______________________________________________

16. When was the last time you felt proud of yourself? Write how you felt.

_______________________________________________

_______________________________________________

_______________________________________________

_______________________________________________

_______________________________________________

17. Write a letter to your past self expressing compassion for their inner struggles.

18. Think of the last time you struggled with self-acceptance and write a compassionate letter to yourself.

Merge all parts of you and accept every aspect of your personality. Integrate your light and dark sides and embrace your flaws. Practice self-compassion and be kind to yourself.

# Section 5: AUTHENTICITY

# Step Into Your True Self

Who are you, really? This is a simple question, isn't it? Well, think again. Most people think they know their true selves. However, when you have been suppressing a part of you for so long, you may not be aware of various aspects of your personality. You may be oblivious to what you are capable of or your true potential.

When you are authentic, you can live a care-free and fulfilling life.[6]

Now that you have integrated your light and shadow self, you are ready to live an authentic life. You can align your values with your lifestyle, overcome your fears, and ignore societal expectations to live a fulfilling life.

This chapter explains the concept of authenticity and provides prompts to help you live your life according to your core beliefs, embrace vulnerability, overcome expectations, and honor your passions.

# What Is Authenticity?

Authenticity is self-determination and self-awareness that aligns your actions, decisions, and lifestyle with your core values, beliefs, and inner truths. Living an authentic life can have a huge impact on your mental, emotional, and physical health. It is a priority for your well-being – like food, water, and sleep. You drink water because you listen to your body's needs. Similarly, being authentic fulfills your emotional needs.

An authentic person lives in the moment, is fully aware of their internal experience, and understands their emotions, thoughts, and behavior. They constantly reflect on whether their actions and reactions align with their psychological needs and values. Authentic people understand the many aspects of their personality and make sure that their lifestyle aligns with each one of them.

Multiple philosophers had different interpretations of the word "Authenticity." German philosopher Martin Heidegger said that authenticity is accepting who you truly are and living up to your full potential. French existentialist Jean-Paul Sartre said that people are free to be whoever they want and interpret their experiences however they like. Danish philosopher Søren Kierkegaard described it as breaking free from societal and cultural restraint.

According to Brené Brown, authenticity is a choice that you have to make every day. Either wear a mask and be someone you are not, or be yourself and let the world see the real you. She stated that authentic individuals accept themselves for who they are. They are aware of their imperfections and share them with no shame or judgment.

Authentic people dare to be vulnerable and imperfect. They aren't ashamed of their deep thoughts and emotions or afraid of letting others see their flaws or mistakes. They know that they are worthy of love and acceptance for who they truly are, not for who they pretend to be.

Who is the real you? To answer this question, you must reflect on your most honest and aligned self. Imagine your life when you are unapologetically yourself. Your words, clothes, actions, etc., reflect your authentic self, not what others expect from you. You don't think of other people's opinions when picking an outfit or making a decision.

However, being authentic is different from being perfect. You don't try to be someone who doesn't make mistakes or always says and does the right thing. You simply live your life in a way that feels true and meaningful to you, which usually means taking risks and making mistakes.

Authentic people know they are flawed and don't pretend to be perfect versions of themselves.

According to psychologist Dr. Carl Rogers, a person can't change or move away from their true self until they accept who they are. He introduced the concept of congruence, which is the harmony between one's inner experience and outward expression. It's when your emotions, thoughts, and physical sensations align with each other.

Congruence is being authentic and transparent around people. You present yourself honestly and openly without lying or pretending to be someone you aren't. You share your true feelings and thoughts without fear of judgment to create genuine and trusting relationships with others. When you are real and honest, people will feel comfortable around you and open up to you.

Authenticity is like a smile. It invites everyone in the room to reciprocate the same behavior.

# Prompts and Questions

The prompts and questions in this section help you identify your true values, passions, and purpose while addressing fears or obstacles you may face while trying to be authentic.

### Living in Alignment with Core Values

Identify the values and principles that are most important to you.

1. What values are most central to who you are?

_______________________________________________

_______________________________________________

_______________________________________________

_______________________________________________

_______________________________________________

_______________________________________________

_______________________________________________

_______________________________________________

2. How can you ensure your actions and choices reflect these values?

_______________________________________________

_______________________________________________

_______________________________________________

_______________________________________________

_______________________________________________

3. What is the first thing that comes to mind when you hear the word "Values"?

_______________________________________________

_______________________________________________

_______________________________________________

_______________________________________________

_______________________________________________

4. Mention the last time you were aligned with your values.

_______________________________________________

_______________________________________________

_______________________________________________

_______________________________________________

_______________________________________________

5. Write down your top five values and mention why they are important to you. Reflect on how these are currently being honored (or neglected) in different areas of your life.

_______________________________________________

_______________________________________________

_______________________________________________

_______________________________________________

_______________________________________________

6. How do these values align with your choices and lifestyle?

_______________________________________________

_______________________________________________

_______________________________________________

_______________________________________________

7. Which areas of your life don't align with your values?

_______________________________________________

_______________________________________________

_______________________________________________

_______________________________________________

8. What makes you feel fulfilled?

_______________________________________________

_______________________________________________

_______________________________________________

_______________________________________________

9. What issues make you angry?

_______________________________________________

_______________________________________________

_______________________________________________

_______________________________________________

10. Are you living in alignment with your values today?

_______________________________________________

_______________________________________________

_______________________________________________

_______________________________________________

11. What happens when you neglect your values?

_______________________________________________

_______________________________________________

_______________________________________________

_______________________________________________

12. What can you do to be in alignment with your values?

_______________________________________________

_______________________________________________

_______________________________________________

_______________________________________________

_______________________________________________

13. What three changes can you make to live according to your values?

_______________________________________________

_______________________________________________

_______________________________________________

_______________________________________________

_______________________________________________

14. If you could change one thing about the world, what would it be? Why?

_______________________________________________

_______________________________________________

_______________________________________________

_______________________________________________

_______________________________________________

15. Mention someone you admire for their values and why.

_______________________________________________

_______________________________________________

_______________________________________________

_______________________________________________

_______________________________________________

16. Mention a book that inspired you to question your values.

_______________________________________________

_______________________________________________

_______________________________________________

_______________________________________________

_______________________________________________

17. If you could change one thing about yourself, what would it be and why?

_______________________________________________

_______________________________________________

_______________________________________________

_______________________________________________

18. What did you learn from your most painful experiences?

_______________________________________________

_______________________________________________

_______________________________________________

_______________________________________________

_______________________________________________

**Embracing Vulnerability and Courage**

Explore the role of vulnerability in living authentically and how you can find the courage to express your true self.

1. In what areas of your life are you holding back your true self?

_______________________________________________

_______________________________________________

_______________________________________________

_______________________________________________

_______________________________________________

2. What small steps can you take to show up more authentically?

_______________________________________________

_______________________________________________

_______________________________________________

_______________________________________________

_______________________________________________

3. Do you struggle with being vulnerable around others? Why?

_______________________________________________

_______________________________________________

_______________________________________________

_______________________________________________

_______________________________________________

4. Are there people you are comfortable being your truest self around? Why?

_______________________________________________

_______________________________________________

_______________________________________________

_______________________________________________

_______________________________________________

5. Why aren't you comfortable around others?

_______________________________________________

_______________________________________________

_______________________________________________

_______________________________________________

_______________________________________________

6. How do you find the courage to be your authentic self?

_______________________________________________

_______________________________________________

_______________________________________________

_______________________________________________

_______________________________________________

7. What steps do you take every day to live an authentic life?

_______________________________________________

_______________________________________________

_______________________________________________

_______________________________________________

_______________________________________________

8. What or who holds you back from expressing your true self?

_______________________________________________

_______________________________________________

_______________________________________________

_______________________________________________

_______________________________________________

9. What does being authentic mean to you?

________________________________________________

________________________________________________

________________________________________________

________________________________________________

________________________________________________

10. When was the last time you struggled to express your true self? Why did you feel this way?

________________________________________________

________________________________________________

________________________________________________

________________________________________________

________________________________________________

11. When was the last time you were in alignment with your authentic self?

________________________________________________

________________________________________________

________________________________________________

________________________________________________

________________________________________________

12. Who were you with? How did you feel?

________________________________________________

________________________________________________

________________________________________________

________________________________________________

________________________________________________

13. What gave you the courage to be open and honest?

________________________________________________

________________________________________________

________________________________________________

________________________________________________

________________________________________________

**Overcoming External Expectations**

Reflect on societal, familial, or peer pressures that might be holding you back from authenticity.

1. What expectations have you internalized from others?

<br><br><br><br><br>

2. How can you begin to prioritize your own truth over external validation?

<br><br><br><br><br>

3. Did your parents set unrealistic high standards for you? How do you deal with them?

<br><br><br><br><br>

4. Do you struggle with being your true self due to peer pressure or society's expectations?

<br><br><br><br><br>

5. Do you dress or speak differently around certain people? Why?

6. When was the last time you didn't express your opinion out of fear of being judged? What went through your mind during that moment?

7. What do you think would happen if people saw the real you?

8. Why do you care about other people's opinions?

9. Who are you when no one is around? Which person do you like better: the private one or the public one?

10. Write a letter to your future self, imagining what your most authentic life looks like and what steps you will take to get there.

## Discovering and Honoring Passions

Explore what truly excites you and how you can incorporate these passions into your life.

1. What activities or experiences make you feel alive and connected to yourself?

2. How can you incorporate these into your daily or weekly routine?

3. Do you have a hobby that you keep private out of fear of being judged? What makes you feel this way?

4. Mention three hobbies that give you joy.

5. If money wasn't an issue, what would you be doing now?

6. If someone hired a private detective to follow you, what would they say you spend your time doing?

7. What is your biggest passion?

8. What makes you feel your best self?

9. What is your favorite place in the world?

10. What activity makes you lose track of time?

11. Describe your perfect day.

12. Describe something or someone that makes you feel like a child again.

_______________________________________________

_______________________________________________

_______________________________________________

_______________________________________________

_______________________________________________

13. Think of the last time you laughed from your heart; what were you doing?

_______________________________________________

_______________________________________________

_______________________________________________

_______________________________________________

_______________________________________________

14. If you could live anywhere in the world, where would that be? Why would you want to live there?

_______________________________________________

_______________________________________________

_______________________________________________

_______________________________________________

_______________________________________________

15. What activities did you enjoy doing as a child?

_______________________________________________

_______________________________________________

_______________________________________________

_______________________________________________

_______________________________________________

16. What was your dream career as a child?

_______________________________________________

_______________________________________________

_______________________________________________

_______________________________________________

_______________________________________________

17. What would you do if you couldn't fail?

_______________________________________________
_______________________________________________
_______________________________________________
_______________________________________________
_______________________________________________

18. What do you regret not trying?

_______________________________________________
_______________________________________________
_______________________________________________
_______________________________________________
_______________________________________________

19. Picture your perfect life. Who are you with, and what are you doing?

_______________________________________________
_______________________________________________
_______________________________________________
_______________________________________________
_______________________________________________

20. What goals would you accomplish now if you had the time and resources?

_______________________________________________
_______________________________________________
_______________________________________________
_______________________________________________
_______________________________________________

21. Create a vision board to visually represent your authentic life, including your dreams, values, and goals.

Your true self is your best self. Love and nourish it. Have the courage to share it with the world. If someone doesn't like you, it's their problem, not yours. Don't let people's opinions or judgments influence who you want to be.

# Conclusion

Embracing your shadow self can be challenging. Many people struggle to make peace with their past mistakes and trauma. Instead of confronting their weaknesses and darkness, they choose to hide and ignore them. They are afraid of being judged or misunderstood.

You can't live your life hiding from your true self. Everyone has parts of themselves that they are embarrassed by and wish they could keep private. However, confident and mentally strong individuals embrace their shadow selves. They find no shame in expressing their emotions and showing their vulnerable side.

The book took you on a journey to explore yourself and meet your true self. It explained the concept of the shadow self and the significance of acknowledging and confronting the hidden aspects of your personality. You should be brave enough to face your emotions, experiences, and beliefs.

Confronting the shadow self may feel like a punishment. However, it will help set you free from your past traumatic experience.

Your inner wounds can scar and traumatize your shadow self. You can't avoid pain for the rest of your life, but you can nurture your broken parts and heal. The book explained the importance of accepting, embracing, and healing your emotional wounds.

You can recover from your trauma and move on from unhealthy relationships and bad experiences. Healing doesn't mean that you have forgotten your past. You can heal while still holding onto the lessons from your past mistakes. You learned to use the prompts in the book to transform your pain into power.

Many people have limiting beliefs that make them feel they aren't good, strong, or smart enough. These prevent them from recognizing their true potential and living a fulfilling life. The book explained that these negative thoughts can hinder your growth. Using the journal prompts, you were able to reframe your limiting beliefs.

You can't heal your shadow self or grow without self-acceptance. You learned how you can accept your dark side and light side, strengths and weaknesses. You can embrace every part of yourself without judgment.

Creating a balanced relationship between both sides of your personality can help you become whole and achieve peace.

The last part of the book answered the question, "Who is the real you?" You learned how to accept your authentic self and live with courage and vulnerability.

You finished the book, but your self-exploration journey isn't over. Keep learning about yourself, healing, and growing. Continue embracing and loving your shadow self, and you will notice a change in your mental and emotional health.

# Part 2: Shadow Work Workbook

*Activities, Techniques, and Meditations to Unravel Your Secret Self, Heal Past Traumas, and Reclaim Your Power*

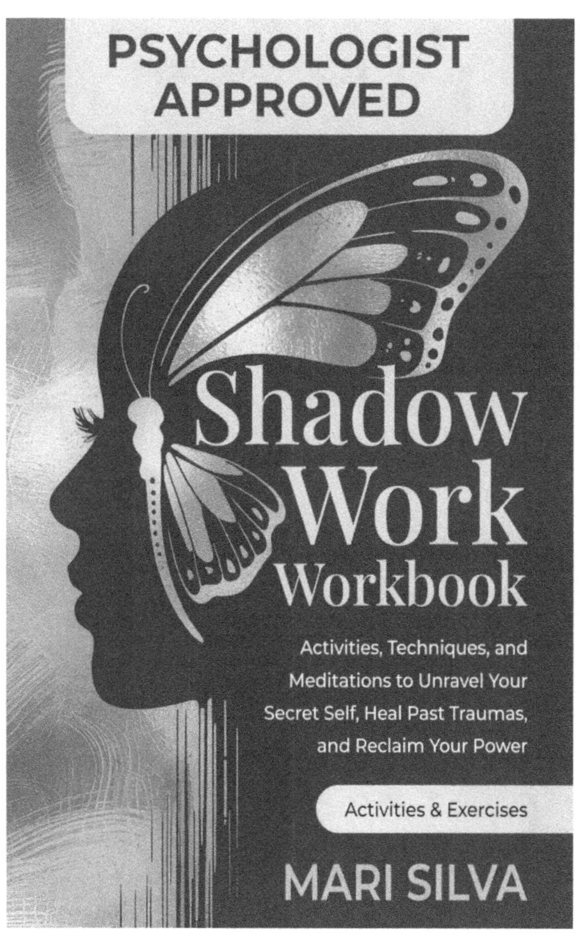

# Introduction

Each person has parts of themselves that they struggle to accept. Perhaps you don't like that you have low self-esteem or that you occasionally lie to get your way. Instead of confronting and working on these issues, you reject and hide them, pretending they don't exist.

However, no one can escape who they are. Everything you bury inside becomes a dark shadow accompanying you wherever you go. It takes over and controls every aspect of your life. When you try to run from it, it catches you, making you feel like a prisoner of something you can't recognize or see.

Everyone has a dark or *shadow* side. While some reject it, others acknowledge it and use it to heal, grow, and become better people.

The book begins by explaining the concept of the shadow and what it represents. You will also learn Carl Jung's role in developing this theory.

The shadow self is born from repressed past experiences and childhood issues. Accepting and embracing every part of yourself allows you to thrive and grow.

Do all shadows look the same? Do you think you have the same shadow as your best friend or partner? Learning about your shadow archetype will give you insight into its traits and the hidden aspects of your unconscious mind.

Have you ever wondered why some situations or people evoke an emotional reaction from you? Understanding your triggers and how they manifest will help you learn more about your hidden wounds.

When you can't confront parts of yourself, you project them onto others. This can lead to misunderstandings, conflicts, and relationship trouble. You must be more self-aware and recognize when you point your finger at someone instead of looking within.

Acknowledging and letting go of suppressed emotions can help you find your path to healing and self-acceptance. You will begin to see your shadow as a part of your authentic self instead of an aspect of your personality that should be hidden.

The last part of the book provides daily exercises that you can incorporate into your routine to overcome challenges and maintain balance between your light and dark sides.

Each chapter contains helpful information and various practice exercises that will help you become more acquainted with your shadow self.

### Key Takeaways

- The book focuses specifically on Shadow Work from a practical aspect.

- It's great for beginners new to Jungian theory and practice.

- It includes practical, hands-on methods from various therapy approaches and modalities (Mindfulness, Jungian Therapy, CBT, Gestalt, etc).

- It incorporates techniques that require writing/drawing and creative expression and techniques you can do without having the book on hand.

- It includes a routines chapter and a bonus worksheet section to supplement those routines.

# Chapter 1: Understanding the Shadow and Shadow Work

Do you love yourself? Think hard before your answer. Loving yourself requires embracing every aspect of your personality, the good, the bad, and the ugly. You don't choose which parts to love; you accept every part of yourself, including your flaws, weaknesses, and dark side.

However, some people reject aspects of their personality that represent parts they don't like or struggle to accept. They spent their lives refusing to acknowledge specific patterns in themselves, leading to resentment. If you ignore your darkness, you will never appreciate your light or be your true self and will live with a false identity.

Your shadow self is an aspect of your personality that deserves to be seen, not shunned. [7]

Every person has a side of themselves they wish didn't exist. However, you can't escape from who you are. All people are a combination of a light side and a shadow side.

Accepting both aspects of your personality will bring you peace and fulfillment.

This chapter introduces the concept of the shadow self, explains why people repress parts of themselves and explores how shadow work can uncover hidden emotions, beliefs, and strengths. It also provides exercises to get you started with shadow work.

## What Is the Shadow?

According to renowned psychiatrist, psychotherapist, and psychologist Carl Jung, the shadow self is a part of your unconscious mind, and he described it as "the thing a person has no wish to be." The shadow self represents the aspects of your personality you repress and struggle to accept or confront. These could be parts you deem evil, dangerous to others, socially unacceptable, harmful to your mental health, or weaknesses and flaws you can't tolerate.

Jung explained that people aren't as good as they believe they are. Everyone has a shadow that threatens the ideal image they have created for themselves. The shadow self often has needs and urges that can conflict with your light side. The contrast between your self-image and your shadow leads you to reject it and project its traits onto others. The characteristics you dislike in someone else can reflect the parts you hate about yourself.

Some believe that the shadow self is the root of all evil. However, this is a misconception. The shadow self can represent your skills, abilities, and negative and positive qualities such as assertiveness, confidence, or intelligence. For instance, some women may pretend to have low self-esteem so they don't intimidate male romantic partners. They hide this significant aspect of their personality, which, if embraced, can help them navigate life challenges, achieve their career goals, and handle any social situation with grace.

You won't live up to your full potential if you don't embrace your shadow self. Say you associate assertiveness with selfishness. You will continue denying this aspect of your personality and allow others to push you around. This can lead to anger, resentment, and guilt. Over time, these negative emotions and unexpressed assertiveness become part of your shadow self.

Your shadow self may also represent your dark side, the part of yourself you are ashamed of and hide from the world. It can be a traumatic experience you can't heal from or a desire you can't satisfy. In his *book Aion: Researches into the Phenomenology of the Self,* Jung explored his own shadow self. He found it to be the most inferior part of the self, bringing shame, guilt, disgust, remorse, fear, compassion, humility, and grief. This reflects the powerful impact of the shadow and the different emotions it evokes.

*The Strange Case of Dr. Jekyll and Mr. Hyde* perfectly represents the battle between one's light and dark sides. Henry Jekyll had an evil personality named Edward Hyde. Jekyll recognized that Hyde was his shadow side, so he tried to suppress it. This resulted in an inner conflict, and eventually, the darkness took over.

Jung's work helped people identify the shadow self as a highly emotional, violent, and primal part of themselves. As a result, they unconsciously keep it private. He also stated in his book that people often judge others on the qualities they reject in themselves. This shows that you can separate yourself entirely from your shadow self without realizing it.

You won't find peace and become whole unless you acknowledge and accept your shadow self. Repressing any part of your personality will impact your relationship with yourself. The more you hide it, the more it controls your behavior and actions. Jung believed that denying one's shadow self can result in various behavioral and mental problems. Over time, you can become unpredictable and harm others and yourself.

The most dangerous part of the shadow self is that it exists in the unconscious mind. It can control your emotions, thoughts, behavior, actions, and reactions. Many people spend their lives unaware of their shadow's impact on their lives. You may lash out at your loved ones for no reason, reject your desires, get defensive, or allow your ego to create false narratives to satisfy and validate the shadow. You may resent your loved ones or feel unsatisfied in your personal and professional life. This can lead to serious issues such as substance abuse or depression.

Your shadow self isn't evil or immoral. It is a part of your identity, and you can't detach yourself from it. If you don't understand its significance, you will treat it as an enemy, causing inner conflicts and hostile behavior. Say you are kind and empathetic. You are understanding towards other people's needs and always know what to say to make them feel better. However, like anyone, you can get irritated or angry. Instead of feeling or expressing these emotions, you hide this part of yourself. You believe they don't fit your calm nature, so you suppress these feelings. However, these emotions are part of the human experience and should be acknowledged and expressed.

If you don't provide a healthy outlet for them, they will come out in the most inappropriate ways. For instance, one day, during a simple disagreement at work, you lose your temper and start yelling at everyone. This is a sign that your emotions can't stay hidden any longer. They are like a volcano and will erupt when you least expect it.

If you don't provide a healthy outlet for your emotions, they will come out in the most inappropriate ways. [8]

Oftentimes, people feel ashamed or upset when they recognize their shadow self. They feel shocked for having the characteristics they have been criticizing in others and for failing to see their true selves. Although this can be difficult, bringing both aspects of your personality together is necessary.

According to Jungian analyst Joseph Lee, the shadow self exists in a dark place with your fantasy, restrained instinct, drive, and forbidden desires. Giving in to it will give you relief and show you who you truly are. Your shadow self shouldn't be feared or repressed. If you embrace it, you will learn who you are and what you could be.

## The Shadow Self, the ID, and the Ego

Understanding the shadow self requires you to familiarize yourself with the id and ego. The id is the primal part of the self that develops from birth. It represents your impulses, desires, anger, instant gratification, and your need for companionship, shelter, and food. Sigmund Freud describes it as an inaccessible and dark part of the self. Conversely, the ego is developed over time as one grows up, matures, and gains experience. It represents the version of yourself you share with the world, including your beliefs, values, and experiences.

The ego is a socially acceptable part of you and often behaves appropriately. This is unlike the id, which only seeks pleasure and avoids pain. The ego prevents the id from making decisions based on impulse and instant gratification and aligns itself with one's values and beliefs.

However, the ego will try to find a balance between satisfying your desires and appropriate behavior. It may distort your reality to create a narrative to validate the id's desires. For instance, you ate a large pizza and convinced yourself you deserved it for eating healthily last week. This can become a pattern of behavior where you make up stories to fit your narrative.

During childhood, the id controls your actions. You only seek pleasure and instant gratification. Some people mature and learn they can't act on every impulse or avoid pain and sadness. Others only focus on satisfying their desires and deny their pain, traumatic experiences, and negative emotions. Living a healthy life and finding harmony within oneself requires fully embracing your id and ego and understanding that both sides make you whole.

The shadow self is the gap between the id and the ego. When you struggle between the image the ego portrays so you can fit in the world and the desires your id pushes you towards, you unconsciously create the shadow self.

Jung explains that the answer to the question, "Who are you truly?" lies in knowing and embracing the shadow self.

# Why Do You Repress Parts of Yourself?

Have you ever wondered why people repress parts of themselves? What would the world be like if everyone acknowledged and accepted every aspect of their personality?

Repression is when you unconsciously block negative thoughts or emotions, unpleasant memories, desires, and impulses. Sigmund Freud described it as a defense mechanism to prevent feelings of anxiety or guilt. It is a temporary solution that can calm you down and reduce the impact of intense emotions.

Freud compared the human mind to an iceberg. The top is the conscious mind, and the part under water symbolizes the unconscious mind. Although you aren't always aware of what goes on in your unconscious mind, you can feel its impact on your behavior, thoughts, and every other aspect of your life. He described repressed emotions as being buried alive. They don't die and will find their way to the surface in the ugliest ways.

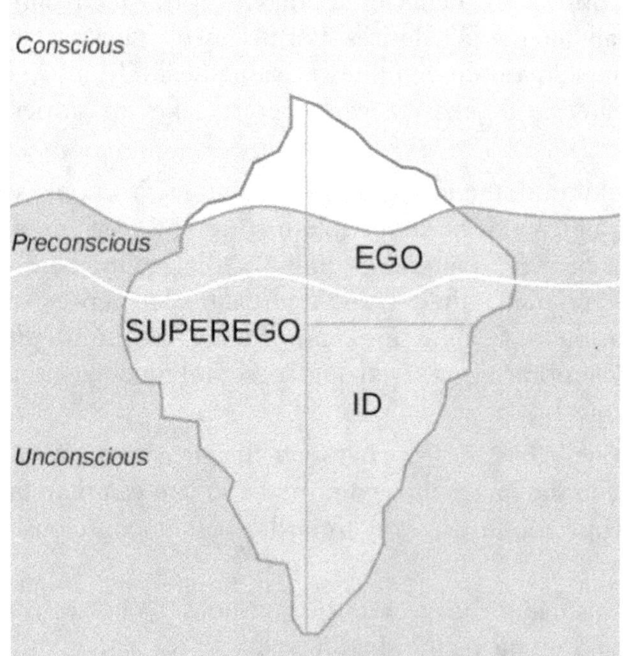


**Freud's psychoanalytic theory of personality.** [9]

While working with patients to help them tap into their unconscious emotions, Freud discovered that the mind hides unwanted thoughts and developed the theory of repression. He believed that people repress their thoughts when they can't confront certain memories, traumatic experiences, thoughts, or emotions, which can lead to serious consequences. Repression can cause depression, anxiety, and stress. However, confronting and accepting these thoughts can help you react to stressors healthily and deal with your problems instead of avoiding them.

Early experiences, such as parental criticism or cultural norms, can drive you to hide emotions or traits that are deemed unacceptable. If you grew up in a home without expressing your thoughts and emotions, you will struggle with being your true self.

Perhaps your parents yelled at you when you cried, so you learned to hide your grief. Or maybe you enjoyed making jokes as a child, but your parents kept telling you not to be silly. You grew up believing that being funny is wrong, and you hid this side of your personality and became a serious person who rarely laughs.

Children internalize their parents' words and teachings. They hide the parts of themselves that their parents don't approve of, and the emotions they are taught are unacceptable. Suppose your family, community, or society shames you for having certain emotions, opinions, or ideas. In that case, you repress them to protect yourself from judgment and rejection.

Your parents are your first role models. You learn from them how to speak, act, and behave. If they don't express their emotions or avoid dealing with their feelings, you will become ashamed of your negative emotions as well.

Societal expectations and cultural norms also play a huge role. Some people are free-spirited and prefer to live without the constraints of social conventions. However, society or their families may pressure them to get married and have kids or have a nine-to-five job instead of working freelance or on small projects. These individuals end up repressing this side of their personality and giving in to society's demands. They can become resentful for having to live a life that doesn't reflect who they are.

Traumatic childhood experiences can also cause repression. Children who grew up with parents who neglected their needs, didn't validate their emotions, or ignored their accomplishments repress these parts of themselves in adulthood.

Intense emotions can be overwhelming. Some people don't know how to deal with grief, heartbreak, or other painful emotions, so they repress them.

### Signs of Repression

- Struggling to talk about your feelings and thoughts.
- Getting defensive when someone brings up certain topics.
- Feeling numb.
- Distracting yourself with drinking or spending hours on social media.

### Repression Vs. Suppression

Many people use repression and suppression interchangeably. While they are both defense mechanisms, they have different meanings. Suppression is a conscious decision to forget or avoid thinking about traumatic experiences or painful memories. You deliberately ignore all the emotional baggage you can't handle until it no longer crosses your mind.

Say you break up with your partner. Instead of grieving the end of your relationship or sharing your pain with a friend, you choose to suppress these feelings. Perhaps you weren't taught to express your sadness, or you are worried people will deem you weak if you cry. You suppress your emotions and distract yourself from experiencing pain. Some may resort to unhealthy coping mechanisms like drinking, while others may focus on their careers or friendships.

You also avoid talking about your ex-partner and avoid anyone or anything that reminds you of them. While this can help you move on from the relationship, it's only a temporary solution. You can't escape from your pain. Eventually, these suppressed emotions will reveal themselves in the form of mood swings, crying, irritability, anger outbursts, or physical symptoms such as headaches, tense muscles, insomnia, or indigestion.

**Repressed emotions find their way back to you.**[10]

Conversely, repression is unconsciously pushing away unpleasant and overwhelming emotions, thoughts, desires, and impulses. When traumatic experiences or aspects of your personality make you feel ashamed, guilty, or afraid, your mind represses them to protect you. You can't confront these emotions or parts of yourself, so your mind moves them away from your awareness. However, they don't disappear. They exist in your unconscious mind, impacting your well-being, relationships, actions, and behavior, and becoming your shadow self.

Imagine your co-worker telling you that they got promoted. You smile and congratulate them, but deep down, you feel jealous. This is your shadow comparing your achievements with your coworker and triggering feelings of jealousy. Perhaps you are insecure and resent people who achieve their goals before you.

It doesn't matter how deep you bury these emotions. When something triggers the shadow, it always rises to the surface.

# Benefits of Shadow Work

Shadow work involves tapping into your unconscious mind to discover your repressed emotions and the rejected aspects of your personality. You practice specific techniques like meditation to meet your shadow self and uncover the parts of yourself that you have hidden. According to Carl Jung, acknowledging and accepting one's shadow self helps bring all parts of oneself together and achieve wholeness.

He added that confronting the shadow self can help reveal who you truly are, allowing you to understand and learn about yourself. You will access your full, untapped, and unique abilities when you embrace every part of you.

### Brings Transformation and Growth

Confronting and accepting your shadow self helps you uncover your hidden abilities, skills, and talents. Shadow work will bring to the surface all aspects of your personality that you have hidden out of insecurity and fear. This can change how you see yourself and the world around you. You will become more excited about the future and ready to embrace any new opportunities. Your newfound confidence will drive you to make better decisions that will help you grow and transform your life.

### Provides Emotional Healing

Your shadow self can result from a traumatic experience, unvalidated emotions, or neglected needs. Shadow work can help you confront your pain and heal emotionally. You will learn to deal with your anxiety, shame, guilt, or fear instead of repressing or suppressing them so they can no longer influence your self-image and view of the world. As a result, you will become more compassionate, tolerant, and accepting of yourself and the people in your life.

However, this requires you to embrace your shadow self without judgment and bring it to your conscious mind. This will help you react more healthily to your emotional triggers.

### Increases Self-Awareness

Acknowledging the hidden parts of yourself will increase your self-awareness. Shadow work will help you confront the darkest parts of yourself to understand your behaviors, desires, and motivations better. When you are aware of every aspect of your personality, you can live a more authentic life and make decisions that align with your new views and true self.

### Boosts Your Self-Esteem

Confident people acknowledge and embrace every aspect of their personality, including their darkest and most unpleasant sides. You will stop hiding the parts of yourself that you are ashamed of or don't like. You will accept yourself for who you are and understand that every person has weaknesses, flaws, and secret desires. This will give you the courage to live the life you have always wanted and achieve your goals.

### Gives You Clarity

You will never know your true self or your real emotions if you keep hiding the parts of yourself that you don't like. Shadow work reveals your different thoughts, feelings, and desires to help you understand your actions and behavior.

### Makes You More Compassionate

When you make peace with your shadow self, you will stop projecting your insecurities onto others, judge them harshly, or criticize them. Their flaws, weaknesses, and personality traits won't trigger you. You will view people differently and become kinder and more compassionate. You will stop seeing the reflection of your dark side in them. Instead, you will see them as human beings with vulnerabilities and inner conflicts.

### Improves Your Well-Being

Repression can cause various mental and physical problems. You may not be aware that these issues stem from your shadow self until you confront your dark side. Shadow work won't just help you deal with unhealthy patterns of behavior or anxiety but will tackle the root causes to help you heal completely.

### Reveals Your Hidden Talents

Your shadow self doesn't only include painful memories, trauma, or dark desires and traits. It can also include your talents, inner strengths, and other positive qualities to help you thrive. Shadow work can help reveal this part of yourself and unlock all your amazing qualities.

### Teaches Self-Acceptance

Shadow work can help resolve your inner conflicts and bring you self-acceptance. You will no longer experience self-loathing and feel the need to hide parts of yourself. Embracing your shadow allows you to be self-compassionate and treat your dark and vulnerable parts with kindness and understanding.

### Have Better Relationships

You can only have healthy relationships and learn to accept others when you make peace with your shadow self and can love and embrace your light and dark sides. Letting go of judgments and projections can help you see your loved ones for who they truly are instead of a reflection of your shadow self. This allows you to build genuine, loving, and strong relationships.

### Improves Your Creativity

The greatest poets, artists, and writers create masterpieces when they tap into their dark side. English novelist Charles Dickens had a rough childhood. His father went to prison, and he had to work from a very young age. Instead of repressing his harsh experiences, he used them to inspire his novels. Dutch painter Vincent van Gogh suffered from depression for most of his life. He portrayed his emotional pain in many of his paintings, giving them more depth.

You will find many other examples throughout history and modern times. Shadow work can help you tap into your dark self and use these raw emotions in your creative endeavors.

### Enhances Mindfulness and Emotional Intelligence

Shadow work helps you be more present, self-aware, and in tune with your thoughts, emotions, and behavior. This helps improve communication skills and your emotional intelligence, making you more empathetic and able to control your emotional reactions.

### Confront Your Trauma

You won't heal from your past if you keep avoiding it. You need to bring these issues to your consciousness to begin healing. Shadow work can help you confront your traumatic experiences and painful memories. You will learn to accept and move on from your past to become more resilient and emotionally balanced.

# Preparation and Tools Needed

To be mentally, physically, and emotionally prepared, you will need various tools and techniques before you begin shadow work,

### Decide if You Need a Therapist

Before you begin your journey, you should decide whether you will seek a therapist's help or will be able to do shadow work on your own. While you can benefit from professional guidance, you can easily practice these techniques without help. You need to choose what's best for you.

### Recognize Your Shadow

Your shadow can reveal itself through daily interactions or impact aspects of your life. Pay attention to your habits and behavior. Do you have bad habits that hold you back in life? Are there negative patterns of behavior that show up when you interact with people? Do certain places, people, or situations trigger you? These can be signs that your shadow self wants to be acknowledged.

### Explore Your Childhood

You need to think back to your childhood before you begin shadow work. Reflect on how your parents or society reacted when you expressed emotions like sadness or showed certain aspects of your personality. Did they punish you, forcing you to repress these aspects of yourself?

### Meditate

Meditation, breathing exercises, and other mindful techniques can help you connect with your shadow, remain calm when intense emotions arise, and accept yourself without judgment.

### Pay Attention to Your Dreams

Carl Jung believed that dreams can connect you to your unconscious and provide insight into your shadow self. Pay attention to the emotions, characters, and events you experience in your dreams. Write them down as they may reveal secrets about your inner self. You should also focus on your recurring dreams. There is a reason your unconscious keeps sending you the same messages, and you need to uncover it.

### Choose the Right Location

You can't do shadow work while watching TV. Find a quiet and comfortable space that allows you to focus and self-reflect. Close the door, turn off your phone, and eliminate any distractions. Create a positive and inviting environment that lets you be calm and relaxed while embarking on this journey.

### Keep a Journal

Write down in your journal the thoughts and emotions you experience while engaging in shadow work. You can also use it to record your dreams. Reading your journal can help reveal secrets about your shadow and unconscious mind.

### Be Honest with Yourself

You should have the courage to recognize your dark personality traits and unpleasant behavior without shame or guilt. Be brutally honest about who you are and embrace the parts that make you uncomfortable.

### Prepare Yourself Mentally

Open yourself to self-exploration and be prepared for what you will discover. Expect that you may confront the darkest aspects of your personality or recognize your wasted potential. This won't be easy, so refrain from judgment and be kind to yourself!

# Practical Exercises:

In this part, you will practice exercises that will prepare you with shadow work.

### Preparation Checklist

Organize a journal, pens, and any grounding aids like essential oils or calming music to create a shadow work "toolkit." You can also write down a list of supportive practices to use when you feel overwhelmed.

### Mindful Breathing Practice

Before beginning shadow work, practice some mindful breathing techniques to recognize how you feel and learn to relax and center yourself.

### Two-Four Breathing Technique

Instructions:

1. Inhale while counting to two.
2. Exhale while counting to four.
3. Repeat ten times.

### Deep Breathing Technique

Instructions:

1. Put one hand on your stomach.
2. Take a long, deep breath for three seconds.
3. Feel the air filling your belly, and your hand rises.
4. Hold your breath for two seconds.
5. Exhale for three seconds.
6. Feel the air released from your body and your hand falling.
7. Repeat ten times.

### Sighing Breathing Technique

Instructions:

1. Take a long, deep breath through your nose.
2. Breathe out through your mouth while sighing deeply. You can also sigh loudly if you like.
3. Repeat ten times.

### Oceanic Breathing Technique

Instructions:

1. Open your mouth wide.
2. Take a long, deep breath through your mouth.
3. Exhale through your mouth and feel your stomach cave in.
4. Keep your breathing slow and steady.
5. Repeat ten times.

## Nasal Breathing Technique

**Instructions:**

1. Breathe in through your nose.
2. Feel the air filling your belly.
3. Breathe out through your nose and feel the air emptying your lungs.
4. Repeat until you feel more relaxed.

## 4-7-8 Breathing Technique

**Instructions:**

1. Lie down or sit in an upright position.
2. Breathe out and release the air from your body.
3. Inhale through your nose while counting to four.
4. Hold your breath for seven seconds.
5. Exhale while counting to eight through your mouth.
6. Repeat for five minutes.

## Counting Breathing Technique

**Instructions:**

1. Pay attention to your mood, whether you are feeling relaxed, stressed, or anxious.
2. Set your timer for ten minutes.
3. Relax and breathe normally.
4. Count each time you inhale from one to five.
5. Count each time you exhale from one to five.
6. Repeat for ten minutes.

## Mindful Breathing Technique

**Instructions:**

1. Sit in a comfortable position on a chair or a cushion on the floor.
2. Keep your back straight and rest your hands on your knees, or place them beside you.
3. Move your tongue to the roof of your mouth.
4. Let your body relax and pay attention to your physical sensations.
5. Notice how your feet connect to the floor below you and how the chair or cushion feels against your body.

6. Feel the tension released from your body each time you exhale.

7. Breathe normally and focus on the rhythm of your breathing.

8. Feel the air as it enters and exits your body.

9. Feel it in your nostrils, throat, chest, stomach, and abdomen.

10. Notice the sensation of each breath you take.

11. Your mind may wander off, and you may experience different thoughts. This is normal.

12. Observe your thoughts without judgment, let them pass, and refocus on your breathing.

13. Stay in this position while breathing for ten minutes.

14. Allow your body to relax more deeply.

**Balloon Breathing Technique**

**Instructions:**

1. Sit comfortably with your back straight.

2. Close your eyes and focus on your breathing.

3. Imagine that you have a balloon in your stomach.

4. Each time you inhale, the balloon inflates; it deflates each time you exhale.

5. Feel how your abdomen rises and falls every time you breathe in and out.

6. Let any distracting thoughts pass without judgment and refocus on your breathing.

7. If emotions, noise, or physical sensations distract you, acknowledge them and bring your attention back to your breathing.

**Triangle Breathing Technique**

**Instructions:**

1. Sit comfortably with your spine straight.

2. Breathe deeply and only focus on your breathing.

3. Imagine an upside-down triangle with the horizontal base on the upper end.

4. Breathe in while counting to four.

5. Imagine that you go up the triangle with each breath you take.

6. Hold your breath while counting to four and visualize that you are going through the base of the top of the upside-down triangle.

7. Breathe out while counting to four, and imagine that you go down the other side of the triangle.

8. Repeat for a few minutes.

## Anchor Breathing Technique

### Instructions:

1. Imagine that you are on a boat feeling calm, relaxed, and safe.

2. The boat's anchor keeps you where you want to be. You feel secure and happy.

3. Like boats, your body also has anchors that keep it focused.

4. Your lungs, chest, belly, mouth, and nose keep you grounded.

5. Place your hand on your chest and breathe deeply.

6. Exhale slowly.

7. Feel your chest rise and fall.

8. If thoughts distract you, bring your attention back to your anchors.

## Breathe Upon a Star Breathing Technique

### Instructions:

1. Spread your palm out like a star.

2. Trace the outline of your right hand with your left index finger.

3. Breathe in while tracing up from the tip of your wrist to the tip of your thumb.

4. Breathe out while tracing down the other side of your thumb.

5. Repeat, on the other hand.

## Blow Out the Birthday Candles Breathing Technique

### Instructions:

1. Spread your fingers and pretend that each one is a birthday candle.

2. Take a deep breath and slowly exhale as if you are blowing out birthday candles.

3. Lower a finger each time you exhale.

4. After you finish blowing on your five fingers, repeat on the other hand.

**Bumble Bee Breath Breathing Technique**
**Instructions:**

1. Imagine you are a bumble bee.
2. Take a long, deep breath through your nose.
3. Slowly exhale while buzzing like a bee.
4. Place your palms around your ears to amplify the vibration and sound of your buzzing.
5. Repeat a few times.

**Emotional Reactions Log**

Record the moments when you feel triggered or upset throughout the week.

------------------------------------------------------------

------------------------------------------------------------

------------------------------------------------------------

------------------------------------------------------------

------------------------------------------------------------

------------------------------------------------------------

------------------------------------------------------------

------------------------------------------------------------

------------------------------------------------------------

------------------------------------------------------------

------------------------------------------------------------

------------------------------------------------------------

------------------------------------------------------------

------------------------------------------------------------

------------------------------------------------------------

Your shadow self isn't your enemy. It is a part of you that you can't separate yourself from. Acknowledge, confront, and embrace it. Don't suppress or repress your thoughts, emotions, and desires. Every part of you makes you special. Remember to treat yourself with kindness and compassion.

# Chapter 2: Meeting Your Shadow

Are you ready to meet your shadow self? This chapter explores the different shadow archetypes to help you identify your shadow traits. When you understand this side of your personality better, you will become whole and begin a journey of healing, emotional growth, and self-acceptance.

Understand your shadow self through archetypes. [11]

# Shadow Archetypes

Shadow archetypes are sub-personalities that you unconsciously create to protect yourself from trauma and painful experiences. Each archetype has its own coping mechanisms, beliefs, desires, and fears. Like people, these archetypes are different. They have their own personality, voice, unmet needs, and unresolved pain.

Jung's archetypes symbolize various universal themes that evoke strong emotions. They usually manifest in daily interactions, dreams, fairy tales, and myths. The archetypes act as blueprints for the human mind, shaping one's conscious and unconscious thoughts, emotions, perceptions, desires, relationships, actions, and behaviors. They protect one's deepest desires and true identity. Your archetype influences your unconscious mind and helps you understand human psychology and personality.

Carl Jung identified 12 archetypes that offer a deeper insight into your shadow.

### 1. The Ruler

The ruler is also known as the king or tyrant. This archetype is obsessed with power and control and will resort to extreme and immoral behavior to remain in power. These individuals usually make unrealistic demands of others and become furious when people don't cater to their needs. They are prone to destructive behavior and losing their temper.

They become real tyrants when they are in control and will never relinquish it to someone else. If your archetype is the ruler, you will often feel overwhelmed. This is a sign that you need to let go of your need to control everything and let someone help you.

You usually pretend that you know everything. A ruler archetype will never admit that they don't have the skills or knowledge to finish a task out of fear that it undermines their authority.

### 2. The Caretaker

The caretaker is also called the healer, maiden, mother, and queen, and they are people pleasers. This archetype puts all their time, effort, and energy into fulfilling other people's needs while neglecting their own. As a result, they lose their sense of self. They are usually described as victims since they sacrifice everything for others. The caretakers struggle with saying no and setting boundaries.

If you are a caretaker, you will live your life for others and feel guilty when you can't cater to someone's needs. You will feel bitter and resentful when you keep giving and get nothing in return. The caretakers often project their repressed guilt onto others. You may guilt-trip people to fulfill your needs.

You feel overwhelmed during tough situations. You struggle with finding solutions and may feel unworthy and incompetent. This can be the result of an unhealthy childhood when your parents made you feel that you weren't good enough. Or maybe they spoiled you and shielded you from the real world and its problems.

Caretakers constantly feel ashamed and guilty and struggle with having fun and relaxing.

### 3. The Everyman

The everyman is also called the victim, realist, and orphan. This archetype can't handle feeling ignored. These individuals often seek vengeance against those who reject or upset them. If you are an everyman, you probably feel helpless and depend on others. You follow your family and friends' lead and conform to society's expectations. The everyman is a people pleaser. You do as others say, whether it brings you joy or not.

You don't have goals and rely on others to give you direction. This can lead to anxiety and deny you the opportunity for emotional and spiritual growth. Over time, you get tired of being like everyone else and seek individuality.

### 4. The Creator

The creator is also called the visionary, inventor, innovator, architect, and artist. This archetype is a perfectionist. They are never satisfied or content with their lives, which can impact their self-development.

### 5. The Divine Child

The divine child is also called the idealist, the innocent, and the healer. Like the creator, people with this personality are also dependent on others. They would rather follow than lead and can be irresponsible. These individuals don't care about injustice and corruption. They don't stand up for what's right, believing it isn't their concern.

If you are a divine child, you never take responsibility for your mistakes or shortcomings. You believe that all your problems are bad luck or someone else's fault. When someone hurts your feelings, you become cold and distant.

These issues may stem from your childhood. Perhaps you had a sheltered life where you never experienced failure. Maybe you were never taught to admit wrongdoing and found it easier to blame others than confront yourself. You also don't work hard for anything – and give up in the face of challenges.

## 6. The Explorer

The explorer is also called the philosopher, detective, rebel, archer, hunter, entrepreneur, revolutionary, and seeker. Some people conform to society's expectations and rules. They don't get out of their comfort zone or try to explore different options. Most children believe what their parents, teachers, or community tell them. They grow up with preconceived beliefs that they never question or challenge. This can lead to destructive habits and limiting beliefs. The people who settle for the life they are given and follow societal norms lead a mediocre existence and will never experience what life has to offer. They become the product of their society with no original thought or idea. These individuals will feel unfulfilled and lost, leading to the appearance of the shadow explorer.

This is one of the most destructive archetypes. It is the result of living a boring life that doesn't excite you or spark your imagination. You may resort to heavy drinking or drugs to escape from your boring reality or to rebel against societal norms. You may also seek dangerous adventures to get an adrenaline rush.

People with this archetype are consumed with the fear of missing out and often feel restless. They jump from one experience to the next without accomplishing anything or getting satisfaction.

## 7. The Hero

The hero is also called the survivor, athlete, and rescuer. Although this archetype stands up for what they believe in, they may sell out their beliefs out of loyalty to a friend. Most shadow hero individuals had teachers or caregivers who made them feel that they weren't good enough, unworthy of love – or didn't accept parts of their personality. Growing up with people who made them feel like failures and lowered their self-esteem made them believe they had to work hard to earn others' approval and love.

The hero archetype drives them to be reckless and push their limits to prove to themselves and others that they are strong, smart, brave, etc, even if it could get them hurt or killed.

Most shadow hero individuals had caregivers who made them feel that they weren't good enough.[12]

People with the hero archetype do not grow or evolve in life. They don't learn their lessons and believe that their circumstances result from bad luck instead of wrong decisions. As a result, they are considered one of the most immature archetypes.

If you have this archetype, you probably gravitate towards physical instead of emotional connection. You may stay in a relationship with someone you don't love or keep going to an ex-partner for lust.

You are easily tempted and struggle with thinking rationally or controlling your impulses. Consequently, you make rash decisions without planning or considering the consequences. Instead of taking risks, you prefer to stay in your comfort zone and depend on others to make decisions for you.

## 8. The Philanthropist

The philanthropist is also called the destroyer, the father, and the outlaw. This archetype is stubborn, arrogant, impatient, and agitated. Their desire for recognition and power makes them selfish, irrational, and dictatorial. They are stubborn when they want something and must have it, no matter the cost.

People with a philanthropist archetype can be bad-tempered and intolerant. They would rather complain than find solutions for their problems.

### 9. The Sage

The sage is also called the magician, pope, muse, oracle, wise judge, sorcerer, and wizard. This archetype has three main traits: inability to see the truth, emotional detachment, and supercriticality. Children who were never validated can develop a sage archetype and grow up to be perfectionists. They may also be more analytical than emotional and don't allow themselves to feel their emotions.

People with the sage archetype are extremely arrogant. Nothing is ever good enough for them. They set unrealistic standards for others and expect them to adhere to them.

### 10. The Lover

The lover is also called the addict, maiden, damsel, and hedonist. This is the most repressed archetype among men due to the stigma that men shouldn't cry or be vulnerable. Many young boys were told that "Boys don't cry" or "They shouldn't be sad because they are men." They grow up repressing their sensitive side and are unable to express their feelings.

Children who don't receive emotional support from their parents grow up incapable of love and believing they are unworthy of it. They may also develop abandonment issues, leading to the development of this archetype.

If you have the lover archetype, you may struggle to build healthy relationships, connect with others, and love yourself. The inability to love oneself can result in destructive behavior like addiction to drugs or food. You may also become obsessive and jealous in your relationships or push people away.

The hopeless romantic inside of you is constantly looking for love. This can lead to neediness and depression.

### 11. The Trickster

The trickster is also called the magician, entertainer, joker, and fool. This archetype represents the fun and playful side of one's personality. If it's repressed, it can develop a shadow side that can lead to destructive behavior. You may develop addictive tendencies toward food, alcohol, or sex. Having a trickster shadow can make you immature.

Your head is usually in the clouds, and you are constantly imagining a better life, but you do nothing to achieve your goals.

## 12. The Warrior

The warrior is also known as the outlaw, soldier, knight, and destroyer. This shadow is aggressive, especially when you are being assertive. You can be irrational, reckless, impatient, vengeful, jealous, angry, abusive, and violent. You may also resort to gambling, extreme sports, cheating on your partner, or other destructive behaviors.

Your warrior shadow doesn't trust authoritative figures and gets defensive when someone tells you what to do. You love power and being in control, and you get angry when anyone challenges your authority.

However, this is projecting behavior. Deep down, you don't believe you have the skills or abilities to solve your problems or handle any situation. You can also be selfish and competitive and may walk over others to achieve your goals.

# The Role of Shadow in Personal Growth

You need to change how you feel about your shadow. It isn't a broken part that needs fixing but an aspect of your personality that requires acknowledging, attention, and love. Don't see it as a source of negativity but of self-awareness. Each person has strengths and weaknesses, a dark side and a light side, good and bad qualities. You need to embrace both sides and understand that they make you whole. If you reject any part of yourself, you will always feel that something is missing and may turn to food, alcohol, or drugs to fill the void.

Accepting every aspect of oneself is a sign of maturity and the first step to personal growth. You can't grow if you don't confront your trauma, bad memories, and negative emotions.

Integrating all parts of oneself can make you more understanding and compassionate. You recognize that every person makes mistakes. Instead of getting angry or punishing someone when they slip up, you forgive them because you believe everyone deserves a second chance.

Knowing who you truly are requires you to fully understand your shadow self. You can learn a lot about yourself when you uncover the repressed parts. Your shadow can provide insight into our past, trauma, weaknesses, etc. Once you recognize these parts, you will understand the reason behind your actions and behaviors. You will recognize the impact of your traumatic experiences and work on your healing and moving on from the past.

# Practical Exercises

### Shadow Collage

Gather images, words, and symbols that represent your shadow. These could be things you have suppressed or feared. Create a visual collage that reflects these hidden aspects, either physically or digitally.

### Materials

- Scissors
- Glue
- Art paper, canvas, or cardboard
- Paint brush
- Pens, markers, or pencils
- Coloring pencils or paint

### Instructions:

1. Prepare your canvas and place it on your working space.
2. Choose the images you will use for your collage. You can find images, symbols, or words associated with your shadow in magazines, or you can print them online.
3. Cut out the images using scissors.
4. Arrange them on the canvas and glue each one in its place.
5. Color the background using coloring pencils or paint.
6. You can write relevant words or quotes on your collage.

## Identifying Your Shadow Archetype

What does your shadow look like?

-------------------------------------------------------------------

-------------------------------------------------------------------

-------------------------------------------------------------------

-------------------------------------------------------------------

-------------------------------------------------------------------

How does it act and react?

-------------------------------------------------------------------

-------------------------------------------------------------------

-------------------------------------------------------------------

-------------------------------------------------------------------

-------------------------------------------------------------------

Draw how you envision your shadow self/archetype.

## Dialogue with Your Shadow

Write a conversation between your conscious self and the shadow aspect you have discovered. Give your shadow a name and allow it to speak freely without judgment. Then, respond as your conscious self, offering understanding and compassion.

### Instructions:

1. Find a quiet room with no distractions.
2. Sit comfortably and close your eyes.
3. Take a few deep, slow breaths.
4. Imagine you are walking in a forest.
5. You feel the grass beneath your feet, and the air flows through your hair.
6. You can hear the birds singing in the trees and the wind blowing through the leaves.
7. You see the beautiful green trees around you and smell the flowers.
8. Keep walking and exploring the forest.
9. As you walk, you find someone sitting under a tree.
10. You feel curious and approach them.
11. They look at you, and you immediately recognize their face; it's your shadow self.
12. You sit on the ground opposite them.
13. They feel close and familiar to you.
14. You spend a few minutes in silence.
15. Your shadow looks into your eyes, and you immediately connect.
16. You feel that they want to speak but can't since they have been silent for so long.
17. You decide to start speaking. Ask it, "How are you feeling?"
18. "What have you been carrying all these years?"
19. "What have you been hiding from me and the world?"
20. "Share with me the memories I have forgotten."
21. Imagine how they will answer every question and respond to them.
22. Keep the conversation going until you feel that you have truly known your shadow.

What questions do you want to ask your shadow?

------------------------------------------------------------

------------------------------------------------------------

------------------------------------------------------------

------------------------------------------------------------

------------------------------------------------------------

------------------------------------------------------------

## The (Gestalt) Empty Chair Technique

This is an interesting and potentially more advanced way to meet your shadow, not in a closed-eyes visualization way, but in an actual dialogue setting. In the "Empty Chair" exercise, visualize your shadow self sitting opposite you in a chair. Have a dialogue, expressing your fears and frustrations, then switch roles to respond as the shadow. Reflect afterward by journaling any insights or emotional shifts, focusing on how the shadow can contribute positively to your life.

Your shadow self is your companion. They have been with you throughout your life and know everything about you. Don't be afraid to acknowledge it and get to know it. It will reveal a lot about you.

# Chapter 3: Triggers, Patterns, and Projections

Do some situations or people trigger an emotional reaction from you? Do you project your repressed emotions or personality traits onto others? You may not notice that you feel different when you encounter certain people or events. Most people either brush off these occurrences as a bad mood or don't notice that external factors impact their feelings.

Recognize when you project your repressed issues onto other people. [18]

Triggers, unconscious patterns, and projections shape your emotional experience. Understanding their impact on your personality and daily interactions will provide insight into your shadow.

The exercises in this chapter will help you confront your triggers and recognize when you project your repressed issues onto other people.

# Triggers

Triggers are stimuli that elicit intense emotional reactions such as anger, grief, fear, or guilt. They are a reaction to unconscious wounds or repressed/suppressed emotions. Unresolved issues leave you vulnerable to riggers. A traumatic experience can cause you pain that you can't handle or confront, so you bury it instead of dealing with it.

You may go on with your life, pretending that this situation hasn't happened, convincing yourself that you've moved on from it. However, a song, movie scene, or smell can bring back these emotions you have been trying to avoid. Triggers can come like waves, drowning you in strong emotions.

An event, situation, person, light, sound, scent, sight, or physical sensation can bring up a painful memory of a traumatic experience you may have forgotten about, suppressed, or tried not to think about. For instance, Fireworks and the sounds of explosions in movies can be triggering to soldiers. Someone who had a terrible car accident when they were young may find the sound of a car horn triggering as it can bring back the painful memory and feelings of fear and pain.

Triggers can also be internal. An emotion, a memory, or something inside of you can evoke an emotional reaction. Say you are running, and your heartbeats start to elevate. This can trigger a memory of when your father would come home drunk, yelling, and you would run and hide out of fear. Internal triggers include sadness, pain, traumatic memories, muscle tension, loneliness, anxiety, anger, and feeling abandoned, vulnerable, and overwhelmed.

Many people confuse being triggered with being offended or uncomfortable. However, they have different meanings. Being triggered is finding an event or situation intolerable. In some situations, it can intensify the impact of a traumatic experience or worsen the symptoms of an existing mental health condition like PTSD.

Being triggered can make you feel like you are experiencing the trauma all over again. While some people can cope with stress and bad memories, others can struggle when they hear a sound, smell something, or see someone that reminds them of a painful situation.

Your emotional reactions to triggers may seem justified, but they can seem disproportionate to people unfamiliar with your past. For example, a person may be triggered when their partner doesn't reply to their text messages or forgets to check on them after an important interview. While most people will understand that their partner was probably busy, a person whose parents neglected their emotional needs will be triggered. This simple situation can bring back their childhood trauma, evoking feelings of anger, sadness, and pain.

### Examples of Triggers

- Illness
- Injuries
- Unwanted touching
- Sexual harassment
- Violence in movies, TV shows, or news
- Breakups
- Being ignored
- Rejection
- Loneliness
- Being judged or ridiculed
- Arguments
- Loud noises
- Yelling
- Specific tastes, scents, sights, sounds, or textures
- The holidays
- The anniversary of trauma

# Patterns

Triggers can lead to a pattern of challenging and negative behaviors. You may react negatively to certain situations and kick a chair, yell at someone, hit the wall, scratch and injure yourself, isolate yourself from others, or withdraw from social interactions.

Patterns of behavior can help you recognize when you are triggered and vice versa. Pay attention to your reactions to people, events, places, and external and internal stimuli. Do you binge eat or drink excessively after certain situations or events? Do you withdraw during the holidays? These patterns of behavior can be a reaction to triggering experiences. Notice your unusual behavior after every situation, as it can give you insight into your triggers and shadow self.

Similarly, triggers can also reveal deep-rooted patterns in your behavior. Repression can make you act out of character. You may develop specific behaviors when you fail to acknowledge and accept your emotions. These patterns repeat themselves as a reaction to your unresolved issues and wounded past. They can be dangerous and harm your mental, emotional, and physical health. Some people turn to gambling, drinking, or alcohol to cope.

You will repeat the same behavior if you don't confront and heal your shadow self.

# Projections

Projection is a defense mechanism that allows you to cope with unresolved issues. It involves recognizing your repressed/suppressed emotions or personality traits in others. For instance, you may make fun of a friend for their lack of self-confidence to avoid confronting your own self-esteem issues.

Projection is an unconscious process that usually reflects your actions and behavior rather than the person you are projecting them onto to help ease the intensity of your emotions. Say you're worried about an upcoming performance review at work. Instead of dealing with these emotions, you criticize your co-worker's project. Converting your anxiety into criticism helps ease your repressed insecurity about your performance.

This is an unhealthy and temporary solution to your problems. It helps you manage unpleasant thoughts, emotions, and desires without confronting them. Projection usually occurs when a person sees aspects of their personality in others that they hate in themselves.

Many people find projection easier than confronting themselves. This helps protect their self-esteem and allows them to tolerate certain aspects of their personality. Attacking or mocking another person for making a mistake is easier than looking within and dealing with your shadow.

Projection usually occurs when a person sees aspects of their personality in others that they hate in themselves. [14]

Your behavior towards the person you are projecting onto reflects how you feel about yourself. If you use cruel jokes to mock them, this indicates your frustration and anger at yourself. Attributing your rejected emotions or traits to others helps you feel superior. You believe that you are better than these people and above these emotions and traits.

### Signs of Projection

- Defensiveness
- Accusations
- Being overly-critical

# Practical Exercises

### Trigger Identification

List moments in the past week when you felt particularly triggered. For each trigger, write a brief description of the event and note your emotional reaction. Then, explore the underlying belief or past experience that might be contributing to this emotional response.

| Triggers | Brief Descriptions | Emotional Reactions | Past Experiences |
|---|---|---|---|
|  |  |  |  |

## Pattern Recognition Journal

Identify recurring patterns in your life, such as choosing the same type of partner or responding in similar ways to stress. Write about these patterns and reflect on when they first began, how they manifest, and the emotions associated with them.

## Projection Awareness Exercise

Think of someone you have had strong negative feelings about. Write a list of traits or behaviors you dislike or judge in this person. Then, reflect on how these traits may exist within yourself, either in your conscious or shadow self.

## Meditation

Triggering situations can be overwhelming. This meditation exercise will put you at ease and help you deal with the situation calmly.

### Instructions:

1. Go to a quiet room and eliminate all distractions.
2. Choose a comfortable position. You can lie or sit down.
3. If you are seated, straighten your spine.
4. Place a pillow under your thighs to take the pressure off your back if you are lying down.
5. Take three long, deep breaths through your nostrils and slowly exhale through your mouth.
6. Now, breathe normally.
7. Remain still and feel your chest rise and fall with every breath.
8. If you experience triggering thoughts or emotions, tell yourself, "I am safe, my mind is at peace, and the universe is protecting me."
9. You feel calmer and more steady with every breath you take.
10. Think of a time you were triggered.
11. Recall the experience with all your senses.
12. Notice if there was a distinguished scent, sound, taste, physical sensation, or feeling.
13. Now, relive the experience physically, mentally, and emotionally as if it is happening right now.
14. Notice how you feel inside.
15. Release this image and emotions, and think of a time when something good triggered you. For instance, the smell of cookies can take you back to your childhood when your grandmother would bake delicious cookies for you and your siblings.
16. Allow yourself to go back to this memory.
17. Notice what you see, hear, smell, touch, and taste.
18. How does this memory make you feel inside?
19. Feel this moment as if it is happening now.
20. How do you feel now?
21. Now, think of an unpleasant situation, nothing traumatic.

22. Recall every emotion and physical sensation that was associated with the experience.

23. Allow yourself to sit with the feeling of discomfort for a few minutes.

24. If you feel overwhelmed, remind yourself that you are here now and safe.

25. Allow yourself to feel all the emotions and physical sensations as they are.

26. Tell yourself that whatever you are feeling now can't harm you. They are just feelings or sensations that have no power over you.

27. You are safe now.

28. Your emotions have no power over you. You are the one in control.

29. Your mind can create different reactions to any moment.

30. The situation doesn't tell you how to react; you make the choice.

31. Your triggers can't influence how you feel. You can change how you feel about them.

32. Imagine yourself living your best life.

33. You have made peace with your shadow self and accepted all parts of yourself. Nothing can touch or trigger you now. You are happy and safe.

34. You have found who you really are.

35. Smile and stay with this feeling for a few minutes.

**Change Negative Thoughts**

Recognize negative thoughts and replace them with positive ones. Write down the trigger, and the thoughts it elicits, and then write a positive thought to reframe the negativity.

| Trigger | Negative Thought | Positive Thought |
| --- | --- | --- |
|  |  |  |

Triggers don't have to control your life. Making peace with your shadow self will lessen its influence and help you accept and embrace yourself.

# Chapter 4: Releasing and Reintegrating

Your suppressed emotions and traumatic experiences don't have to control your life. You can release these feelings and free yourself from their shackles. Bring your shadow self to your consciousness to reintegrate it into your awareness. Accept every part of yourself and let go of the limiting beliefs holding you back.

You can release these feelings and free yourself from their shackles.[15]

This chapter explains how to let go of suppressed emotions, the relationship between the trauma and the shadow, the process of reintegrating the shadow, and self-acceptance.

# Letting Go of Suppressed Emotions

Releasing suppressed emotions is one of the most important aspects of shadow work. Holding on to negative feelings can impact your mental health and every aspect of your life. You can never escape your emotions; burying them deep down will only give them more power over you. You may become numb and detached from others and your surroundings.

Over time, you will feel that there is a wall between you and your emotions, making it hard to access them or express your feelings. This can lead to stress, mood swings, irritability, and anxiety.

### Weak Immune System

Suppressing emotions can cause serious physical issues in the long run. It can weaken your immune system, making you vulnerable to illnesses. The emotional stress of burying your emotions can prevent the body from functioning properly, weakening its ability to fight off diseases.

### Relationships Problems

Keeping your feelings from your loved ones can cause conflicts in your relationships. You will struggle with having an honest conversation or communicating properly. This can create an emotional distance, leading to misunderstandings, fights, and resentment.

### Loneliness and Depression

Suppressing emotions can make you feel alone and misunderstood, causing you to be withdrawn and isolated from your loved ones. People who hide their feelings instead of expressing them deprive themselves of connecting with others and establishing emotional bonds. Over time, they can feel lonely.

Yearning for human connection can cause depression, making it even harder to express your emotions.

### Anger Outbursts

You can't suppress your emotions for long. Eventually, they will reveal themselves at the most appropriate time and way. A simple argument or disagreement can cause severe emotional reactions such as crying or anger outbursts. The emotions you have been suppressing have finally come out at once, and you can't control them. This can confuse your loved ones, leaving them wondering what they did to warrant this reaction.

Suppressed emotions have power over you. They can control your feelings, behavior, and reactions. You become unpredictable and will not know how you will react at any moment. Acknowledging and releasing your emotions can free you from these patterns of behavior and help you heal.

# Understanding Trauma and the Shadow

Dealing with a traumatic experience isn't easy, and for some, it can be impossible. Many people struggle with confronting their past or accepting what happened to them. Your trauma can lead to suppressed emotions or unexplained and unpredictable behaviors and emotional reactions.

Your powerful emotions can be complex to handle. Instead of expressing them to lift the weight off their shoulders, you suppress them and pretend they don't exist.

Suppressed trauma and emotions don't disappear. They lurk in the darkest side of yourself and create your shadow self. This can influence your reactions, fears, and patterns of behavior.

When you don't have a healthy emotional outlet for your traumatic experience, it becomes a prisoner in your body, causing stress and muscle tension. Your past doesn't go away when you avoid talking about it and bury your emotions. It is part of your journey and experience.

Acknowledging and releasing your trauma and reintegrating your shadow into your consciousness can make you aware of your emotions and the impact of your trauma on your mental, emotional, and physical health.

You need to face your past, no matter how scary and traumatizing it was. It's the only way to move on and make peace with your shadow self.

# Reintegration of the Shadow

Reintegration of the shadow is a process that involves bringing your hidden parts to your consciousness. Once you become aware of your shadow self, you can acknowledge and confront it instead of rejecting it.

**You will never be whole unless you embrace every aspect of yourself.** [16]

Shadow reintegration means accepting your trauma, suppressed emotions, flaws, weaknesses, and negative thoughts as part of who you are. You will never be whole unless you embrace every aspect of yourself.

Carl Jung described shadow reintegration as the unification of the conscious and unconscious parts of the psyche. It helps you be more real, grounded, and able to access your creative energy. Each part you integrate reduces your stress, tension, and anxiety, bringing you closer to your true self and being whole. Over time, you will notice a positive change as you become less angry and more understanding and compassionate to people and yourself.

However, shadow integration isn't easy. It is a long journey that will take you to the darkest parts of yourself. It will make you uncomfortable, sad, guilty, and angry. You will need to experience these suppressed emotions to resolve your emotional issues and find peace and balance within yourself.

# Self-Acceptance and Healing

Having a shadow self is a clear sign of a lack of self-acceptance. You reject and hide parts of yourself because you don't want them to define or be associated with you.

You don't want people to see you as a trauma survivor or recognize your flaws and weaknesses. However, everyone has their own demons. Your co-worker may be trying to get out of a toxic relationship, your best friend may be working to overcome their childhood trauma, and your cousin may be struggling with self-esteem issues.

While some people accept their problems and deal with them to heal, others struggle with accepting them, thereby creating a shadow self.

Self-acceptance requires you to change how you view your shadow self. It isn't a broken part that needs fixing but an integral part of your authentic self that should be embraced and loved. You need to reconcile with your shadow and have a healthy relationship with it to be able to love and accept yourself.

# Practical Exercises

### Visualization – Releasing Suppressed Emotions

Visualize yourself sitting in a peaceful place, holding a bag filled with suppressed emotions. Feel its weight and then imagine releasing the bag into a safe space, allowing yourself to feel lighter and freer.

Draw the visualization.

**Releasing Affirmations Exercise**

Repeat these affirmations daily, particularly when you feel triggered. You can also write your own on a lined page or in your journal/notebook.

------------------------------------------------------------

------------------------------------------------------------

------------------------------------------------------------

------------------------------------------------------------

------------------------------------------------------------

------------------------------------------------------------

------------------------------------------------------------

------------------------------------------------------------

------------------------------------------------------------

------------------------------------------------------------

------------------------------------------------------------

------------------------------------------------------------

------------------------------------------------------------

------------------------------------------------------------

------------------------------------------------------------

------------------------------------------------------------

------------------------------------------------------------

------------------------------------------------------------

------------------------------------------------------------

- I release what no longer serves me.
- I forgive myself and embrace my shadow.
- I am not scared of the future.
- I let go of my worries; I know these negative thoughts aren't true.
- I am loved and at peace.
- I allow myself to rest and heal.
- I forgive myself for all the feelings I didn't allow myself to feel.
- I am not fighting myself anymore.

- I can feel my emotions without judgment.
- My past doesn't define me.
- I embrace peace and release resentment.
- I am stronger than my problems.
- I don't see challenges; I only see opportunities.
- I allow myself to heal.
- I let go of my anger and embrace peace.
- I release any negative energy.
- I give myself time to heal.
- I can get through anything.
- I let go of my past traumatic experience.
- I let go of pain and welcome love.
- I embrace love and leaving.
- My shadow self and I are working in harmony.
- I am healing with every breath I take.
- My past has no power over me.
- I release my past regrets and focus on the present.
- I welcome new beginnings and let go of old patterns.
- I am free of past limited beliefs.
- I forgive myself and lead a guilt-free life.
- I become more compassionate when I forgive myself.
- I forgive myself for unconsciously destroying my peace.
- I am ready to live as who I am.
- I am moving on from my mistakes.
- I release the grip my trauma has on me.
- I accept that I am human and I make mistakes.
- I let go of my guilt and shame.
- I forgive myself to set myself free.

### How to Set Affirmations

1. Sit in a quiet place with no distractions.
2. Take a few deep breaths to calm down and focus.
3. Set intentions and decide what you want your affirmations to be about.
4. Think of three to five affirmations that reflect your emotional state, and write them down.
5. Visualize your affirmations becoming a reality.
6. Believe every word you say and feel the emotions behind them.
7. Repeat them every day.

### Trauma Release Exercise (TRE)

Trauma Release Exercises (TRE) are stretching exercises that focus on the muscles of the lower body and can help release tension and trauma. They encourage natural neurogenic tremors, which are muscle spasms, to regulate the nervous system and release stress. Reflect on your experience while practicing these exercises. Understand that healing through TRE is gradual and personal. Be patient and give yourself time.

**DISCLAIMER: You must work with a therapist in the case of severe trauma, like abuse.**

You should create a calm, quiet environment to practice these exercises.

### TRE Exercise #1 Stretch for Upper Legs

**Instructions:**

1. Lie down on your back.
2. Bend your knees with your feet flat on the floor and right underneath you.
3. Open your knees and bring the soles of your feet together. Tuck your heels to your body.
4. Lift your hips off the floor for 30 seconds, then bring them down and rest for another 30 seconds.
5. Slowly bring your knees close together, two inches closer in increments.
6. Pause for two minutes.

**TRE Exercise #2 Stretching to Open the Front of Your Body**

1. Stand with your feet hip-width apart.

2. Look up and put your hands behind you.

3. Bend your knees slightly, push your hips forward, and bow your back to stretch your muscles.

4. Rotate your hips and pelvis to one side, but don't change the position. Take five slow, deep breaths.

5. Bring your feet to the center.

6. Widen your stance and rotate in the opposite direction while maintaining the same position.

**TRE Exercise #3 Hip, Pelvis & Upper Leg Stretching**

1. Stand and spread your legs about shoulder-width apart.

2. Bend your knees while folding your body forward, hang your neck and head down, and touch the floor with your hands. Your hands should be in the center of your feet.

3. Remain in that position.

4. Take four slow, deep breaths.

5. Relax and let the tension be released from your body.

6. Slowly move your hands to one foot.

7. Hang on the floor.

8. Remain in this position and take four slow, deep breaths.

9. Move your hands to the other foot and stretch.

10. Hang on the floor.

11. Remain in this position and take four slow, deep breaths.

12. Move your hands to the center and bring them between your legs behind you.

**TRE Exercise #4 Wall Sitting Stretch for Upper Legs**

1. Sit with your back against the wall.

2. Remain in this position for five minutes.

3. Return to a standing position.

4. Bend your knees and lean your body forward.

5. Touch the ground with your hands and remain in this position for one minute.

### TRE Exercise #5 Upper Leg Stretching

1. Stand and put one leg in front of the other.
2. Lower your hips as if you are about to sit down and bend your front knee.
3. Bend and straighten your knee on your front leg ten times.
4. After you finish, shake your leg and repeat the previous steps on the other leg.

### TRE Exercise #6 Calf Stretching

1. Place one foot in front of you and put your weight on it.
2. Your back leg should remain on the floor for balance.
3. Lift your front heel, then put it back down.
4. Repeat six times.
5. After you finish, shake your leg.
6. Repeat the previous steps with the other leg.

### TRE Exercise #7 Ankle Stretching

1. Stand up with your feet shoulder-width apart.
2. Roll onto the sides of your feet and sway.
3. Stand on the inside of one foot and the outside of the other.
4. Remain in this position for a few seconds, then sway to the other side.
5. Sway in each direction six times.
6. Shake your feet after you finish.

### TRE Exercise #8 TRE Spiral Visualization Technique

1. Sit comfortably and close your eyes.
2. Take long, slow, and deep breaths.
3. Think of a traumatic experience.
4. Run a quick body scan and try to identify any tingling, pressure, stress, tension, pain, or any other sensation.
5. Visualize a spiral turning in the area where you recognize the sensation.
6. Notice if the spiral turns fast or slow.
7. Visualize pulling the spiral inside out.
8. Continue deep breathing until the spinning slows down and becomes less intense.

9.  Open your eyes and bring your awareness to your surroundings.

10. Do another body scan exercise to see if the physical sensation has changed.

N.B. The next chapter includes step-by-step instructions for the body scan meditation.

## Meditation – Embracing/Integrating the Shadow Self

Focus on bringing a shadow aspect into conscious awareness. Imagine a golden light filling them with warmth as you embrace this aspect. Write about your experience, and include a "Last Letter to My Shadow" based on this technique.

### Instructions:

1.  Lie down, sit, or stand.

2.  Close your eyes and relax your face and body.

3.  Imagine the stress and tension exiting your body each time you exhale.

4.  Breathe in slowly and breathe out gently.

5.  Feel the air as it moves through your body like a river.

6.  It fills you with peace and tranquility.

7.  Focus on your breathing and let any distracting thoughts pass without focusing on them.

8.  Tell yourself that your past mistakes, trauma, and suffering have only made you a stronger and better person.

9.  You have known defeat but have managed to get out of the darkness to the light.

10. Now, you are stronger, wiser, more gentle, and compassionate.

11. You accept every part of yourself because the darkness has made you wiser.

12. Explore your thoughts without judgment.

13. You are who you are. The sooner you accept it, the happier you will be.

14. Repeat these affirmations while breathing slowly:

    o  *I am worthy of love and acceptance. I am worthy of love and acceptance.*

    o  *I accept myself just as I am. I accept myself just as I am.*

- o *I am growing and learning every day. I am growing and learning every day.*
- o *I forgive myself for past mistakes. I forgive myself for past mistakes.*

15. Now, imagine a warm light surrounding you. It represents love, compassion, and self-acceptance.

16. It envelops your body, filling you with comfort and warmth.

17. This light is healing you from negative thoughts and self-doubt.

18. It makes you calmer.

19. Stay with this feeling for a few minutes.

20. Now, slowly open your eyes and engage with your surroundings.

Dear Shadow Self,

## Jungian Therapy Reintegration Techniques

### Active Imagination

**Instructions:**

1. Sit at a quiet place indoors or outdoors with no distractions.

2. Think of a recent dream and get a pen and paper to analyze it.

3. Take slow, long, and deep breaths through your nostrils and exhale through your mouth.

4. Keep breathing until you feel calm.

5. Focus your attention on the dream for as long as you can.

6. If your mind wanders off, take a deep breath and bring your attention back to the dream.

7. Your unconscious mind sends you messages through dreams. Analyze the theme, location, symbols, and every aspect of the dream to find what your subconscious mind is trying to communicate to you.

8. Focus all your mental capacities on the dream image until your unconscious mind animates it. This gives your unconscious mind a voice.

9. You may become a part of the dream or speak to one of the characters.

10. This can be difficult if you are focusing on a nightmare, but it is a necessary step to understand your past and emotional state.

11. Engage with the form that appears to you. Make the image as vivid as possible.

12. Draw or write what you experienced.

13. Disengage from the dream and take a break. Go for a walk, watch TV, or think about something else.

14. Go back to what you wrote or drew in your notebook, analyze it, and try to find the hidden meaning behind the dream.

### Gestalt Technique for Reintegrating the Shadow

Write down a part of yourself that you have rejected. Then, place two chairs opposite each other. Sit in one chair and imagine the rejected part sitting in the other. Have a conversation with this part. Say everything on your mind and imagine. Next, switch chairs and respond as the rejected part.

Don't be afraid or ashamed of your shadow. It reflects your experience, what you have endured and survived, and who you can become. Embrace it and reintegrate it into your consciousness. Release your suppressed emotions before they control your reactions and behavior, turning you into someone you won't be able to recognize or love.

# Chapter 5: Becoming Whole Through Daily Routines

Now that you have been familiarized with your shadow self, released your repressed emotions, and embraced every aspect of your personality, you must learn to maintain balance among all parts of yourself. You can't go back to your old ways and reject the aspects of your personality you can't confront.

You need to learn to maintain balance among all parts of yourself.[17]

This chapter includes daily techniques to help you embrace your light and shadow aspects and become whole.

# The Importance of Being Whole
## (Integrated Shadow Awareness in Daily Life)

Being whole involves bringing your shadow self to your consciousness, confronting it, and embracing your repressed desires, fears, and emotions.

### Making Better Decisions

Accepting your shadow self helps you make healthier decisions. When you are aware of your weaknesses and strengths, you can make choices that benefit who you are instead of the false image you have created in your head. Say your partner starts talking to you about getting married. You tell them that you are happy with how things are or that it is too soon, even though you have been together for a long time. While it is normal for partners to talk about their future, you feel they are pressuring you and decide to end the relationship.

However, repression or suppressing parts of yourself made you unaware of some deep issues. Perhaps you don't want to get married due to a fear of commitment stemming from your childhood. Maybe your parents are divorced or had an unhealthy relationship that made you afraid of marriage.

If you were at peace with your shadow self, you could see that your partner wasn't pressuring you. They love you and want to have a future with you. You would have made a better decision instead of ending your relationship.

You could have discussed your commitment issues with your partner and worked through them together, or you could have sought help from a therapist to save your relationship.

### Live Authentically

You can't live authentically if you're ashamed of any parts of yourself. Authentic individuals are proud of who they are and never try to hide their emotions or any aspect of their personality. Embracing your light and dark sides helps you live a genuine life. Becoming aware of your strengths, weaknesses, desires, skills, and abilities improves your life fulfillment and helps you have sincere relationships and honest interactions.

### Personal Empowerment

Being whole and bringing your shadow self to your consciousness increases your resilience, self-worth, and self-esteem, reducing self-doubt. This can empower you, allowing you to navigate and overcome life's challenges.

### Emotional Balance

Accepting your shadow self helps you achieve emotional balance and reduces your inner conflict. This brings inner peace, stability, and emotional regulation.

### Better Relationships

Acknowledging and embracing your dark side helps you understand yourself and others better, which encourages self-acceptance and self-compassion. You will also be able to extend this kindness to others and make them feel seen, heard, loved, and accepted. This can lead to stronger connections and healthier relationships based on respect, mutual understanding, and empathy.

### Preventing Unconscious Projections

Shadow awareness can prevent unconscious projections. When you recognize and accept every aspect of your personality, you don't feel the need to project your weaknesses, flaws, or repressed emotions onto others. Lack of self-acceptance makes you struggle with managing your desires, thoughts, and feelings. Instead of acknowledging them, you criticize these traits in others.

# Balancing Light and Shadow

Embracing all parts of yourself is a journey. You will encounter judgmental people throughout your life or face situations where you set unrealistic standards for yourself. Social norms can also pressure you to be someone you are uncomfortable with or hide parts of yourself to prevent judgment and rejection.

This can make self-acceptance an ongoing battle that doesn't seem to end. Every day, you have a different fight with someone, a fight inside you between your dark and light sides, and a fight outside between who you want to be and what society expects of you.

Some people may think that integration is a one-time event. They believe their work is done once they have accepted their shadow self. However, this is an ongoing process that requires daily practices and rituals.

# The Importance of Living Authentically

Living authentically requires you to express your complete and true self in every aspect of your life.

## Improves Your Mental Health

When you embrace your shadow self, you live authentically, and your thoughts and actions are aligned. You become free from inner conflict and have to live a life according to your beliefs and values. This allows you to engage in healthy behavior that improves your mental health and well-being.

Embracing your shadow self allows you to live authentically and free from inner turmoil. [18]

## Healthier Relationships

Authentic individuals have healthy, deep, and rich relationships. They are honest with themselves and their partners, are aware of their needs, and treat their loved ones with understanding and compassion. Since they are at peace with their shadow themselves, they don't project their repressed feelings or traits on them, resulting in less conflict and confusion in their relationships.

## Boosts Your Self-Confidence

Living according to your own beliefs without worrying about other people's opinions increases your self-confidence. Authentic people trust in their skills and abilities. They understand that every person has flaws and makes mistakes, so they aren't ashamed of themselves. These individuals are aware of their strengths and weaknesses. They know how to use their skills and talents to achieve their goals and what they need to do to improve and grow.

### Freedom to Be Yourself

Authentic individuals don't hide behind a mask. They aren't afraid of other people's opinions. Shadow work reduces your fear of judgment. Knowing every aspect of your personality makes you feel at peace and confident in yourself. You don't worry about what other people think of you. This allows you to live authentically and build deep connections.

# Practical Exercises

### Morning Intention Writing for Shadow Integration

Develop a daily practice of writing a brief morning intention related to your shadow. Reflect on how you wish to engage with your shadow during the day, setting intentions like, "Today, I will approach my shadow with curiosity, not judgment," or "I will remain open to the lessons behind my emotional triggers."

### Mindfulness Check-Ins

Perform brief mindfulness check-ins during moments of tension or "shadow flare-ups." Observe your emotions non-judgmentally and consider whether shadow aspects influence your reactions.

-------------------------------------------------------------------------------

-------------------------------------------------------------------------------

-------------------------------------------------------------------------------

-------------------------------------------------------------------------------

-------------------------------------------------------------------------------

-------------------------------------------------------------------------------

### Daily Active Imagination Exercise

Set aside 10-15 minutes in the morning for active imagination. Close your eyes and bring to mind an unresolved internal conflict or an unfamiliar aspect of your shadow. Visualize this part of yourself as a character or figure and engage in an open, imagined dialogue. Allow this figure to speak freely, responding with curiosity and compassion. Note any insights or emotions that arise and write a summary afterward to reflect on the experience throughout your day.

---
---
---
---
---
---
---
---
---
---

N.B. You can download, print, or copy as many sheets as you want in the bonus section.

## Meditation for Wholeness

Sit quietly each morning and visualize your inner world as a house with many rooms, each representing different parts of yourself. Visit the rooms that feel neglected, dusty, or closed off, symbolizing your shadow. As you imagine opening the door, you can invite light, warmth, and understanding into these spaces, affirming, "I embrace all parts of my being, and every part has a place in my wholeness."

## Daily Shadow Journaling

Write about your shadow interactions, dialogues, thoughts, triggers, and so on. Do this at the same time every day.

---
---
---
---
---
---
---
---
---
---

## Daily Shadow Affirmations

Write down affirmations that integrate your shadow traits.

### Examples of Affirmations

- I accept all parts of myself, even those I find difficult to face. I accept all parts of myself, even those I find difficult to face.

- I am resilient.

- I am worthy of love, flaws and all.

- I am loved.

- I accept every part of me with love.

- I embrace all aspects of myself, even the hidden parts in the shadows.

- I honor the lessons my shadow teaches me as they help me grow and transform.

- I integrate my shadow with love, kindness, and patience.

- I accept that the light can't exist without the darkness.

- I am whole with my light and shadow in perfect balance.

- I no longer suppress parts of myself out of fear of judgment or rejection.

- I let go of my fears and embraced my shadow's lesson.

- Accepting my shadow leads to an authentic life.

- Shadow work rituals create balance between my light and dark sides.

- I embrace imperfections and let go of perfections.

- I am in control of my thoughts and emotions.

- I am free, healed, and whole.

-------------------------------------------------------------------

-------------------------------------------------------------------

-------------------------------------------------------------------

-------------------------------------------------------------------

-------------------------------------------------------------------

-------------------------------------------------------------------

-------------------------------------------------------------------

## CBT-Based Thought Record

At the end of the day, use a simple CBT thought record to reflect on moments when your shadow surfaced.

| A situation and how it made you feel | Negative thoughts you had as a reaction to the situation | Assess the evidence for and against the negative thought | A balanced, realistic thought, and how you feel about it |
|---|---|---|---|
|  |  |  |  |

## Meditation to Live Authentically

**Instructions:**

1. Find a quiet room and eliminate distractions.
2. Sit or lie down. Choose what makes you comfortable.
3. Close your eyes and focus on your breathing.
4. Feel your belly rise and fall with every breath.
5. Take long, deep breaths and exhale slowly.
6. Feel the air filling your lungs each time you inhale.
7. Feel your lungs deflate when you exhale.
8. Drop your shoulders and feel your body soften.
9. Now that you want to live authentically, you must first recognize when you compromised your true self out of fear of judgment or rejection.
10. Think of when you changed or hid something about yourself to gain someone's approval.
11. Acknowledge the experience without judgment.
12. Don't be hard on yourself. Understand that this is part of your journey.
13. Inhale and breathe in light, kindness, and love.
14. Hold them in your body, heart, and every part of you.
15. Each time you inhale, visualize yourself in a white bubble of healing light.
16. Each time you exhale, imagine you are releasing your need to change for someone else, compromise, settle, or justify.
17. Breathe in and tell yourself that you deserve to be loved for who you are.
18. Breathe out and tell yourself to let go of the beliefs that you must hide parts of yourself to be accepted.
19. You are worthy of love. Love yourself and never change for anyone.
20. Forgive yourself for all the times you weren't your authentic self.
21. Let go of judgment and criticism.
22. Keep breathing and feel the weight of every time you compromise or settle lifting out of your shoulders, neck, belly, and cells.

23. Now, all the negativity is released from your body, leaving space for self-acceptance and authenticity.

24. Tell yourself each time you breathe in, "I am free to be myself. I can express myself honestly and openly. I attract people and relationships who love me for who I am."

25. Say, "My authenticity is my greatest strength. I choose to be the real me without fear. I have enough."

26. Take a few long and deep breaths.

27. Focus only on your breathing.

28. Make a commitment to never be afraid to be who you are. Allow the real you to shine and to live an authentic life.

29. You have made peace with your shadow and are free to be your authentic self.

30. Keep breathing and tell yourself, "I am safe, at peace, and whole."

31. Take in this moment and allow yourself to enjoy your newfound freedom to be unapologetically yourself.

32. Now, bring your awareness to reality, take a deep breath, and open your eyes.

## Shadow Work Questions

Ask yourself these questions daily to keep track of your emotional reactions.

1. What did you emotionally react to today?

------------------------------------------------------------

------------------------------------------------------------

------------------------------------------------------------

------------------------------------------------------------

------------------------------------------------------------

2. What was the reason behind this reaction?

------------------------------------------------------------

------------------------------------------------------------

------------------------------------------------------------

------------------------------------------------------------

------------------------------------------------------------

------------------------------------------------------------

3.  Were these emotions the result of a traumatic event?

--------------------------------------------------------------

--------------------------------------------------------------

--------------------------------------------------------------

--------------------------------------------------------------

4.  What did you judge yourself on today?

--------------------------------------------------------------

--------------------------------------------------------------

--------------------------------------------------------------

--------------------------------------------------------------

5.  Why did you judge yourself? Did a parent or teacher use to criticize and judge you as a child?

--------------------------------------------------------------

--------------------------------------------------------------

--------------------------------------------------------------

--------------------------------------------------------------

6.  What did you judge others on today?

--------------------------------------------------------------

--------------------------------------------------------------

--------------------------------------------------------------

--------------------------------------------------------------

--------------------------------------------------------------

7.  Were you projecting your repressed emotions or traits on them?

--------------------------------------------------------------

--------------------------------------------------------------

--------------------------------------------------------------

--------------------------------------------------------------

--------------------------------------------------------------

--------------------------------------------------------------

8.  What are you most afraid of?

____________________________________________________

____________________________________________________

____________________________________________________

____________________________________________________

____________________________________________________

____________________________________________________

9.  What feelings are you trying to avoid?

____________________________________________________

____________________________________________________

____________________________________________________

____________________________________________________

____________________________________________________

10. Why are you afraid of these feelings?

____________________________________________________

____________________________________________________

____________________________________________________

____________________________________________________

____________________________________________________

____________________________________________________

11. What are you most ashamed of?

____________________________________________________

____________________________________________________

____________________________________________________

____________________________________________________

____________________________________________________

____________________________________________________

12. How do you sabotage yourself?

_______________________________________________

_______________________________________________

_______________________________________________

_______________________________________________

_______________________________________________

_______________________________________________

_______________________________________________

13. How do you avoid uncomfortable feelings, thoughts, personality traits, or situations?

_______________________________________________

_______________________________________________

_______________________________________________

_______________________________________________

_______________________________________________

_______________________________________________

14. How are you similar to your parents?

_______________________________________________

_______________________________________________

_______________________________________________

_______________________________________________

_______________________________________________

_______________________________________________

15. Which of your parents' qualities do you try to avoid?

_______________________________________________

_______________________________________________

_______________________________________________

_______________________________________________

_______________________________________________

_______________________________________________

### Pay Attention to Your Dreams

Your dreams can provide insight into your unconscious and shadow self. They can reveal things about yourself you aren't aware of and answer many of your questions. Keep a journal next to your bed and write down your dreams. Analyze them and reflect on patterns, hidden emotions, symbols, and recurring themes.

### Body Scan Meditation

Repressed emotions can cause muscle tension. This meditation helps you check on each part of the body and release stress and any other negative emotions. You can practice every day to check in on yourself and relax. The body scan exercise also increases your self-awareness, making you attuned to your mental and physical states. This helps you recognize your internal signals so you can respond appropriately in any situation. It also makes you mindful, so you are focused on the present moment.

Document your dreams in a dream journal.[19]

### Instructions:

1. Lie down on your bed or floor and get comfortable. You can sit or stand if it makes you more comfortable.
2. Close your eyes and take a few long, deep breaths.
3. Inhale through your nose and exhale through your mouth.
4. Repeat a few times.
5. Focus on your body's movements as you breathe in and out.
6. Ignore your surroundings and only focus on your body.
7. Feel the sensation of the pillow, chair, or floor below you.
8. Start the body scan at the head.

9.  Notice what sensations you are feeling. Do you feel tense, pressure, tightness, tingling, buzzing, high temperature, or neutral? Observe these feelings without judgment.

10. Be open and curious about how you feel. Analyze the sensation. Does it reflect your emotional state? Perhaps your shadow self is making you tense or anxious for a reason. Try to find the source of this sensation.

11. Take a few deep breaths and feel the sensation leave your body each time you exhale.

12. Move to the next body part and repeat the previous steps.

13. It's normal for your mind to wander off, and you may start having distracting thoughts. Observe these thoughts without judgment and then refocus on your body.

14. Keep scanning each body part until you reach your feet.

15. After you finish, take a few slow breaths and open your eyes.

Self-acceptance, releasing suppressed emotions, and reintegrating your shadow self takes time. Your work doesn't end after you finish the book. You must create a daily routine that allows you to be aware of your shadow self, connect with it, and become whole.

# Bonus: 369 Shadow Worksheets

This section includes a variety of useful printable/downloadable sheets that you can use to practice the exercises in the book.

**Trigger Logs**

- https://www.moodcafe.co.uk/media/kpckexdu/1-1-trigger-logs.pdf
- https://cerebral.com/care-resources/trigger-log
- https://davemacdonaldlcsw.com/wp-content/uploads/2010/11/Logs-Trigger-and-Daily-Experiences.pdf
- https://www.moodcafe.co.uk/media/51691/TRIGGER%20LOG%20ANALYSIS%20WORKSHEET.pdf
- https://ssaic.ca/wp-content/uploads/2020/03/Trigger-Log.docx.pdf
- https://sensoryprocessingexplained.com/lesson/preventing-sensory-triggers/sensory-triggers-log-2/
- https://static1.squarespace.com/static/5301a9a9e4b0cb0fd9a9b572/t/6272c5d87da3d168040bd981/1651697112621/TrackingTriggers.pdf
- https://www.therapistaid.com/therapy-worksheet/triggers

## Daily Thought Record Sheets

- https://www.getselfhelp.co.uk/docs/ThoughtRecordSheet7.pdf
- https://www.therapistaid.com/therapy-worksheet/thought-record
- https://thinkcbt.com/images/Downloads/Thought_Records/EXAMPLE-CBT-THOUGHT_RECORD-V-THINK-CBT-01072020.pdf
- https://www.cci.health.wa.gov.au/-/media/CCI/Mental-Health-Professionals/Bipolar-Disorder/Bipolar-Disorder---Worksheets/Bipolar-Worksheet---14---Thought-Diary-3.pdf
- https://assets-global.website-files.com/601807d7eaae5a60d79e8911/611bcc4be9f99ad891b71556_Simple%2BThought%2BRecord.pdf
- https://positive.b-cdn.net/wp-content/uploads/Automatic-Thought-Record.pdf
- https://www.getselfhelp.co.uk/docs/SocialAnxietyThoughtRecordSheet.pdf
- https://positive.b-cdn.net/wp-content/uploads/2020/09/Cognitive-Restructuring-Worksheet.pdf
- https://positive.b-cdn.net/wp-content/uploads/Facts-or-Opinions-Worksheet.pdf
- https://positive.b-cdn.net/wp-content/uploads/Exceptions-to-the-Problem-Questionnaire.pdf
- https://positive.b-cdn.net/wp-content/uploads/Finding-Discrepancies-Worksheet.pdf

## Daily Mindfulness Check-in Sheets

- https://sarahspeaking.com/mindful-worksheet/
- https://www.adorethemparenting.com/5-tips-for-creating-a-mindful-morning-routine-free-printables/
- https://bearable.app/free-worksheets-and-resources/mental-health-worksheet/mental-health-check-in-worksheet/
- https://15worksheets.com/worksheet-category/mindfulness/#google_vignette

- https://www.developgoodhabits.com/mindfulness-worksheets/?epik=dj0yJnU9dUcwNlJlLWZnajR5Sl9GOVRSbUJGM09mdlFqV3dOeTQmcD0wJm49UWtuYkFrc1dZUzBER2NKVEZEMmFsZyZ0PUFBQUFBR2Y3d3dj

## Weekly Meditation Plans Sheets

- https://edit.org/blog/meditation-journal-templates

- https://www.freepik.com/vectors/weekly-plan-meditation

- https://www.etsy.com/listing/1200946409/weekly-meditation-log-printable-weekly

## Shadow Journaling Sheets

- https://seekingserotonin.com/shadow-work-journal-prompts/

- https://www.scribd.com/document/681591286/Shadow-work-Journal-prompts-30-dayshttps://www.scribd.com/document/681591286/Shadow-work-Journal-prompts-30-days

- https://static1.squarespace.com/static/5d02aa4f260aa3000144c909/t/5f9ed86bc0d9fd7d2f8187ba/1604245611753/Shadow+Work+Journaling+Worksheet.pdf

# Conclusion

You can't grow and thrive if you keep rejecting aspects of your personality. Every part of you makes you whole. Your flaws, trauma, past experiences, and weaknesses contribute to who you are. If you repress them, they will overpower you. You shouldn't be ashamed of your trauma or pain. Your scars show that you are a survivor. They reflect your strength and what you can overcome.

You shouldn't hide your flaws and weaknesses from the world. No one is perfect, and if you pretend to be one, people will see through it. Don't try to be someone you are not to gain people's approval or avoid their judgment. No one will accept you if you don't accept yourself. People will love and admire you when you show your true self and embrace your light and dark sides.

The book took you on a journey to the darkest parts of yourself. It introduced you to your shadow self and explained the concept of shadow work. You understood the difference between repression and suppression and why you hide your emotions.

Shadow work is an effective tool for increasing self-awareness and making peace with oneself. Before you practice these exercises, you need to be prepared and create a welcoming environment that will help you focus, self-reflect, and meditate.

Each person has a shadow archetype. You need to identify yours before you bring your hidden side into your conscious mind. Learning about your shadow self can help you grow, heal, and accept yourself. It isn't a broken part that requires fixing; it is an aspect of yourself that needs attention, love, and compassion.

Some people and events can be triggering. You need to be aware of your emotional reactions in every situation, as they can give you insight into your suppressed and repressed emotions. Triggers can also reflect patterns of behavior that you develop when you don't confront your shadow.

Learning about projections will help you recognize when you unconsciously attribute your traits to others. This can make you more self-aware and help you identify your hidden traits and emotions.

Your trauma and shadow are connected. If you don't confront your past experiences, they will manifest as suppressed emotions affecting your mental, physical, and emotional well-being. You need to confront and release your trauma to reintegrate your shadow self into your conscious mind.

Embracing your shadow self and becoming whole is a journey that doesn't end when you finish reading. You need to incorporate the exercises and techniques in the book into your daily routine to be constantly in touch and aware of your shadow self and repressed emotions.

If you enjoyed this book, I'd greatly appreciate a review on Amazon because it helps me to create more books that people want. It would mean a lot to hear from you.

**To leave a review:**

1. Open your camera app.
2. Point your mobile device at the QR code.
3. The review page will appear in your web browser.

---

*Thanks for your support!*

# Here's another book by Mari Silva that you might like

# Your Free Gift
# (only available for a limited time)

Thanks for getting this book! If you want to learn more about various spirituality topics, then join Mari Silva's community and get a free guided meditation MP3 for awakening your third eye. This guided meditation mp3 is designed to open and strengthen ones third eye so you can experience a higher state of consciousness. Simply visit the link below the image to get started.

https://spiritualityspot.com/meditation

Or, Scan the QR code!

# References

**Part 1: Shadow Work Journal**

10 Journal Prompts for Breaking or Overcoming Limiting Beliefs. (2023, April 4). HolisticNiss. https://www.holisticniss.com/blog/overcome-limiting-beliefs

15 Journal Prompts For Self-Compassion. (2021, May 21). Dreaming by Dusk. https://www.dreamingbydusk.com/blog/journal-prompts-for-self-compassion

Alexa. (2022, December 12). 14 Journal Prompts for Limiting Beliefs – Ambitiously Alexa. Ambitiouslyalexa.com. https://ambitiouslyalexa.com/journal-prompts-for-limiting-beliefs/

Alice Miller: The Childhood Trauma: The Zero 5.0laf – The Official Website of Andrew Vachss. (2024). Vachss.com. https://www.vachss.com/guest_dispatches/alice_miller2.html

Bachert, A. (2024, May 9). Cognitive Reframing: 3 Steps to Change Your Perspective. Rula. https://www.rula.com/blog/cognitive-reframing/

Baldwin, M. (2022, March 30). What the New Science of Authenticity Says about Discovering Your True Self. The Conversation. https://theconversation.com/what-the-new-science-of-authenticity-says-about-discovering-your-true-self-175314

Biesalski, C. (n.d.). Shadow Work: What It is and How to Do It > The Essential Guide! CONNI BIESALSKI. https://www.conni.me/blog/shadow-work

Blanchfield, T. (2024, February 7). What to Know About Somatic Experiencing Therapy. Verywell Mind. https://www.verywellmind.com/what-is-somatic-experiencing-5204186

Brem, P. (2023, May 2). Embracing Vulnerability and Self-Compassion for Resilience and Growth. Linkedin.com. https://www.linkedin.com/pulse/embracing-vulnerability-self-compassion-resilience-growth-brem-msc/

Brené Brown – How to Be Yourself. (2014, July 21). Oprah.com. https://www.oprah.com/inspiration/brene-brown-how-to-be-yourself_1

Clover, M. (2023, June 15). 25 Shadow Work Journal Prompts To Discover Your True Self. Molly Clover. https://mollyclover.com/25-shadow-work-journal-prompts-to-discover-your-true-self/

Coelho, S. (2020, May 27). Journaling For Emotional Health: 12 Writing Prompts. Psych Central. https://psychcentral.com/blog/journal-prompts-to-heal-emotions#healing-heartbreak

Congruence and Genuineness in Psychotherapy. (2024, February). Socialworktestprep.com; Social Work Test Prep. https://socialworktestprep.com/blog/2024/february/01/congruence-and-genuineness-in-psychotherapy/?srsltid=AfmBOorK1VRGYuUYjtGJfMTGAV7ZeMYFgMzJa5AtHNZILukd4jaKclqo

Courtney Harris Coaching. (2020, June 23). 12 Affirmations to Use When You Are Facing Self-Doubt -. Courtney Harris Coaching. https://courtneyharriscoaching.com/12-affirming-beliefs-for-getting-out-of-competition-and-into-connection/

Cy, S. (2017, December 24). 22 Thought-Provoking Journal Prompts to Clarify Your Worldview, Increase Your Motivation, and Discover Your Unique Purpose. Medium; The Writing Cooperative. https://writingcooperative.com/22-thought-provoking-journal-prompts-to-clarify-your-worldview-increase-your-motivation-and-aa879f9568c8

Dickeson, L. (2020, June 11). Congruence and Incongruence – How to Believe You're Good Enough | Ranch Hands Rescue. Ranch Hands Rescue. https://ranchhandsrescue.org/congruence/

Dubin, K. (2024, November 20). Healing from Emotional Neglect: Understanding Inner Child Wounds and Reclaiming Emotional Freedom – SWEET INSTITUTE – Continuing Education for Mental Health Professionals. SWEET INSTITUTE – Continuing Education for Mental Health Professionals – the One Stop Shop for Mental Health Clinicians and Agencies. https://sweetinstitute.com/healing-from-emotional-neglect-understanding-inner-child-wounds-and-reclaiming-emotional-freedom/

Fagan, D. (n.d.). Journal prompts & ideas for emotional release. My TMS Journey. https://mytmsjourney.com/resources/journal-prompts-ideas-for-emotional-release/

Friedrich, S. (2023, November 23). Self-Compassion Journaling Prompts: 101 Ways To Be Kinder. Writing by Saskia. https://writingbysaskia.com/self-compassion-journaling-prompts/

Gemma. (2022, May 2). Journaling for Well-being: Your Authentic Self. Gemma Brown Coaching. https://www.gemmabrowncoaching.co.uk/post/journaling-for-well-being-your-authentic-self

Glass, L. J. (2024, August 15). Emotional Blockage: How To Find Release. PIVOT. https://www.lovetopivot.com/what-causes-emotional-blockage/

Green, R. (2023, April 27). How to Live with Authenticity and Be Your Truest Self. Verywell Mind. https://www.verywellmind.com/live-with-authenticity-7483232

Griffiths, N. (2021, January 11). 31 Days of Shadow Work Journal Prompts For Healing and Growth. Seeking Serotonin. https://seekingserotonin.com/shadow-work-journal-prompts/

Hagen, P. (2024, August 21). 47 Journal Prompts for Emotional Awareness – Hagen Growth. Hagen Growth. https://hagengrowth.com/journal-prompts-for-emotional-awareness/

Hammer, B. (2015). Healing Our Emotional Pain and Relationship Pain. Journal of Psychology & Clinical Psychiatry, 2(5). https://doi.org/10.15406/jpcpy.2015.02.00091

Hannah, D. (2024, August 5). Self-Integration: The Important Pathway To Inner Wholeness. Symbosity. https://symbosity.com/how-to-achieve-self-integration/#penci-What_does_it_mean_to_be_self-integrated

Jeffrey, S. (2019, January 11). A Closer Look at Carl Jung's Individuation Process: A Map for Psychic Wholeness. Scott Jeffrey. https://scottjeffrey.com/individuation-process/

Jordan. (n.d.). Understand Your Values and Beliefs with Helpful Journal Prompts. Spirited Earthling. https://www.spiritedearthling.com/mindfulness-and-meditation/understand-your-values-and-beliefs-with-helpful-journal-prompts

Kristen Webb Wright. (2023, October 13). Beyond Perfectionism: 30 Journal Prompts for Self-Compassion. Day One | Your Journal for Life. https://dayoneapp.com/blog/perfectionism/

KW Marketing Team. (2021, January 10). 10 Positive Affirmations to Help You Crush Your Limiting Beliefs. KW Outfront Magazine. https://outfront.kw.com/training/10-affirmations-to-help-you-crush-your-limiting-beliefs/

LaVine, R. (2023, March 28). 100+ Deep Shadow Work Prompts To Accept Yourself And Move Forward. Science of People. https://www.scienceofpeople.com/shadow-work-prompts/

Luoma, J. (2017, October 5). Self-Enquiry into Self-criticism, Self-blame, and Shame. ACT with Compassion. https://www.actwithcompassion.com/self_enquiry_into_self_criticism_self_blame_and_shame

M, S. (2023, December 20). 50 Self-Compassion Journal Prompts for Inner Growth. Little Crystals | Happiness, Harmony, and Balance. https://littlecrystals.com/blogs/news/self-compassion-journal-prompts

Martin, S. (2019, July 19). Reflective Questions to Help You Quiet Your Inner Perfectionist. Psych Central. https://psychcentral.com/blog/imperfect/2019/07/reflective-questions-to-help-you-quiet-your-inner-perfectionist#Shift-your-negative-thinking

Matheka, W. (2023, March 18). Journal Prompts for Inner Child Healing. Wendy Matheka. https://www.wendymatheka.com/post/journal-prompts-for-inner-child-healing

McBride Sr, C. (2023, May 2). Addressing Emotional Wounds: The Hidden Key to Success and Well-Being. Www.linkedin.com. https://www.linkedin.com/pulse/addressing-emotional-wounds-hidden-key-success-christopher-mcbride-sr/

Morin, A. (2023, May 9). How Cognitive Reframing Works. Verywell Mind. https://www.verywellmind.com/reframing-defined-2610419

Neff, K. (2015). Self-Compassion. Self-Compassion. https://self-compassion.org/

Ola, F. (2024, December 26). 100+ Shadow Work Journal Prompts for Healing and Self Discovery. Her Lifestyle Pursuit. https://herlifestylepursuit.com/shadow-work-journal-prompts/

O'Connell, R. (2023, June 1). The Importance of Overcoming Limiting Beliefs (With Examples) | Guider AI. Guider-Ai.com. https://guider-ai.com/blog/overcoming-limiting-beliefs/

Pedneault, K. S. (n.d.). How Accepting Difficult Emotions Can Improve Emotional Health. Very Well Mind. https://www.verywellmind.com/how-accepting-emotions-can-improve-emotional-health-425368#toc-why-accepting-emotions-is-helpful

Penrose, C. (2024, November 13). 50 Shadow Self Journal Prompts. LeStallion. https://lestallion.com/blogs/journal-prompts/50-shadow-self-journal-prompts?srsltid=AfmBOoqhoxUyOUWxdb8uLqAEMeZQmPDrkNA4HpifL6ZSek8WhN-P6-YH

Perry, E. (2022, June 13). 8 Benefits of Shadow Work and How to Start Practicing It. Www.betterup.com. https://www.betterup.com/blog/shadow-work

Perry, E. (2024, February 28). 75 Shadow Work Prompts for Healing, Growth, & Mental Health. Www.betterup.com. https://www.betterup.com/blog/shadow-work-prompts

Psychologs Magazine. (2023, May 16). Carl Jung's Concept of Individuation. Psychologs Magazine | Mental Health Magazine | Psychology Magazine | Self-Help Magazine. https://www.psychologs.com/carl-jungs-concept-of-individuation/?srsltid=AfmBOoqW8ZUALVehRc638r3bBk08f_Yq1GDaVQw

Raypole, C. (2021, May 17). Ready, Set, Journal! 64 Journaling Prompts for Self-Discovery. Psych Central. https://psychcentral.com/blog/ready-set-journal-64-journaling-prompts-for-self-discovery#the-journal-prompts

Recognizing and Coping with Negative Emotions. (n.d.). www.hopkinsmedicine.org. https://www.hopkinsmedicine.org/about/community-health/johns-hopkins-bayview/services/called-to-care/recognize-cope-with-negative-emotions

Resnick, A. (2024, December 6). 25 Questions to Help You Discover Your True Passions. Very Well Mind. https://www.verywellmind.com/25-questions-to-discover-your-passions-8754230

Roy, M. (2024, March 12). 3 Lessons from Brené Brown that Will Help You Embrace Your Authenticity. Medium. https://medium.com/@roymihika06/3-lessons-from-bren%C3%A9-brown-that-will-help-you-embrace-your-authenticity-8910d8d28471

Sandstone Care Team. (2025, February 5). Journal Prompts for Mental Health: Boost Your Well-Being. Sandstone Care. https://www.sandstonecare.com/blog/journal-prompts-mental-health/

Sargeant, K. (n.d.). Getting to Know Your Shadow. The Tools. https://www.thetoolsbook.com/blog/getting-to-know-your-shadow

Saxena, M. (2024, April 26). Self-Integration: 5 Key Principles. Linkedin.com. https://www.linkedin.com/pulse/self-integration-5-key-principles-manasi-saxena-xhdcc/

Schlamm, L. (2014). Individuation. Encyclopedia of Psychology and Religion, 866–870. https://doi.org/10.1007/978-1-4614-6086-2_329

Schroeder, W. (2023, August 23). Somatic Experiencing (SE): Understanding Dr. Peter Levine's Trauma Therapy – Just Mind. Just Mind. https://justmind.org/somatic-experiencing-se-understanding-dr-peter-levines-trauma-therapy/

Sciandra, F. (2019, August 15). 30 Journal Prompts to Explore Your Creativity, Desires, and Passions. Francesca Sciandra. https://francescasciandra.com/blog/30-journal-prompts-to-explore-your-creativity-desires-and-passions

Simone. (2023, March 7). 75 Powerful Journal Prompts For Forgiveness. We Mind Growth. https://wemindgrowth.com/journal-prompts-for-forgiveness/#15-selfforgiveness-journal-prompts

Sonia. (2022, February 5). How Did I Overcome My Limiting Beliefs through Journaling. Aligned Business Alchemy. https://soniamotwani.com/journaling-through-limiting-beliefs/

Starfire, A. L. (2017, May 8). 6 Journaling Prompts to Conquer Your Inner

Critic – Writing Through Life. Writingthroughlife.com. https://writingthroughlife.com/6-journaling-prompts-to-conquer-your-inner-critic/

TalktoAngel . (2024, December 20). Online Counselling | Online Therapy | Marriage Counsellors | TalktoAngel. TalktoAngel. https://www.talktoangel.com/blog/understanding-emotional-blocks-causes-symptoms-and-solutions

Team Asana. (2021, November 29). 10 limiting beliefs and how to overcome them. Asana. https://asana.com/resources/limiting-beliefs

Van, H. (2023, August 9). Limiting Beliefs: How They Hold You Back and How to Break Free. Day One | Your Journal for Life. https://dayoneapp.com/blog/limiting-beliefs/#h-journal-prompts-for-identifying-and-challenging-limiting-beliefs

Villines, Z. (2022, August 30). What is shadow work? Benefits and exercises. Www.medicalnewstoday.com. https://www.medicalnewstoday.com/articles/what-is-shadow-work#benefits

What is Individuation? Carl Jung and the Journey of Self. (2018, March 22). Harley TherapyTM Blog. https://www.harleytherapy.co.uk/counselling/what-is-individuation-carl-jung.htm

Wooll, M. (2022, July 19). Don't let limiting beliefs hold you back. Learn to overcome yours. BetterUp. https://www.betterup.com/blog/what-are-limiting-beliefs

Your "Shadow" Self – What It Is, And How It Can Help You. (2017, September 7). Harley TherapyTM Blog. https://www.harleytherapy.co.uk/counselling/shadow-self.htm

**Part 2: Shadow Work Workbook**

Anchor breathing. (n.d.). https://positive.b-cdn.net/wp-content/uploads/Anchor-Breathing.pdf

Anderson, O. (2024, March 26). 100 Shadow Work Exercises: Making the Unconscious Conscious & Growing Real - Oli Anderson | Coaching for Realness. Oli Anderson | Coaching for Realness. https://olianderson.co.uk/shadowwork/

Attard, A. (2020, November 4). Repressing Emotions: 10 Ways To Reduce Emotional Avoidance. PositivePsychology.com. https://positivepsychology.com/repress-emotions/

Beauman, J. (2019, March 15). Psychological Projection: Dealing With Undesirable Emotions. EverydayHealth.com. https://www.everydayhealth.com/emotional-health/psychological-projection-dealing-with-undesirable-emotions/

Berkeley. (2022, December 18). The Importance of Authenticity. Berkeley Exec Ed. https://executive.berkeley.edu/thought-leadership/blog/importance-authenticity

Body Scan Meditation (Greater Good in Action). (n.d.). Ggia.berkeley.edu. https://ggia.berkeley.edu/practice/body_scan_meditation

Brock, F. (2013, December 31). The Only 25 Affirmations You Need to Forgive Yourself | Prolific Living. Prolific Living. https://www.prolificliving.com/forgive-yourself-affirmations/

Brown, H. (2021, July 5). Fostering Self-Forgiveness: 25 Powerful Techniques and Books. PositivePsychology.com. https://positivepsychology.com/self-forgiveness/#affirmations

Chan, K. (n.d.). What Is Shadow Work, Exactly? Verywell Mind. https://www.verywellmind.com/what-is-shadow-work-exactly-8609384

Cherry, K. (2023, March 16). How Does Repression Work in Our Unconscious Mind? Verywell Mind. https://www.verywellmind.com/repression-as-a-defense-mechanism-4586642

Collier, T. (2024, October 6). Understanding Repressed Emotions: What Lies Beneath. Vicpsychology.com.au. https://vicpsychology.com.au/blog/understanding-repressed-emotions

Cuncic, A. (2023, August 23). What Does It Mean to Be "Triggered?" Verywell Mind. https://www.verywellmind.com/what-does-it-mean-to-be-triggered-4175432

Embrace Your Shadow - Unlock your Creativity - Arielle Schwartz, PhD. (2014, June 8). Arielle Schwartz, PhD. https://drarielleschwartz.com/embrace-your-shadow-unlock-your-creativity/

Goode, J. (2014, May 21). Make Paper Collage Art in 15 minutes - 100 Directions. 100 Directions. https://www.100directions.com/make-paper-collage-art-in-15-minutes/

Greater Good Science Center. (2024). Mindful Breathing (Greater Good in Action). Ggia.berkeley.edu. https://ggia.berkeley.edu/practice/mindful_breathing

Insight Network, Inc. (2025). Insight Timer - #1 Free Meditation App for Sleep, Relax & More. Insighttimer.com. https://insighttimer.com/healingwithemma/guided-meditations/journey-to-your-shadow-guided-visualization

Insight Network, Inc. (2025). Insight Timer - #1 Free Meditation App for Sleep, Relax & More. Insighttimer.com. https://insighttimer.com/catedubois/guided-meditations/meditation-for-being-triggered

Insight Network, Inc. (2025). Insight Timer - #1 Free Meditation App for Sleep, Relax & More. Insighttimer.com. https://insighttimer.com/mccallahan49/guided-meditations/meditation-on-self-acceptance

Insight Network, Inc. (2025a). Insight Timer - #1 Free Meditation App for Sleep, Relax & More. Insighttimer.com. https://insighttimer.com/BreathworkMeditations/guided-meditations/embracing-your-shadow-self_1

Insight Network, Inc. (2025b). Insight Timer - #1 Free Meditation App for Sleep, Relax & More. Insighttimer.com. https://insighttimer.com/barbaradeyo/guided-meditations/living-in-authenticity

Instructables. (2014, September 9). How to Make a Paper Collage. Instructables; Instructables. https://www.instructables.com/How-to-Make-a-Paper-Collage/

Jeffrey, S. (2014, August 13). Jungian Shadow Work: A Beginner's Guide (5 Key Exercises). Scott Jeffrey. https://scottjeffrey.com/shadow-work/#Six_Powerful_Benefits_of_Jungian_Shadow_Work

Jeffrey, S. (2014, August 13). Jungian Shadow Work: A Beginner's Guide (5 Key Exercises). Scott Jeffrey. https://scottjeffrey.com/shadow-work/#What_is_Shadow_Integration

Jeffrey, S. (2014, August 13). Jungian Shadow Work: A Beginner's Guide (5 Key Exercises). Scott Jeffrey. https://scottjeffrey.com/shadow-work/#Five_Powerful_Shadow_Work_Exercises

Keerti. (2023, June 29). Affirmations for emotional release - Keerti - Medium. Medium. https://medium.com/@keertijetly19/affirmations-for-emotional-release-fea3ee662d3d

Lazreg, A. (2023, July 6). The Psychology of Suppression and Repression  – The Crisis of The Modern Man. ILLUMINATION. https://medium.com/illumination/the-psychology-of-suppression-and-repression-the-crisis-of-the-modern-man-c71890894341

Leaf Complex Care. (2023, July 17). What Can Trigger Behaviours That Challenge and How to Prevent Them?  – Leaf Complex Care. Leafcare.co.uk. https://leafcare.co.uk/blog/what-can-trigger-behaviours-that-challenge-and-how-to-prevent-it/

Lonngi, G. (2024). The Jungian Shadow and Self-Acceptance. Tamug.edu. https://www.tamug.edu/nautilus/articles/The%20Jungian%20Shadow%20and%20Self-Acceptance.html

Mikhail, J. (2025, February 8). CBT Techniques for Managing Trauma Triggers. IKON Recovery. https://www.ikonrecoverycenters.org/cbt-techniques-for-managing-trauma-triggers/

Mindful Breathing Exercises. (n.d.). Action for Healthy Kids. https://www.actionforhealthykids.org/activity/mindful-breathing-exercises/

Mindful Breathing. (n.d.). Getselfhelp.co.uk. https://www.getselfhelp.co.uk/docs/MindfulBreathing.pdf

Narbonne, L. (2024, August 12). 100 Letting Go Affirmations to Help You Heal and Thrive. the Innertune Blog | Affirmations, Manifestations & Positivity; The Innertune Blog | Affirmations, Manifestations & Positivity. https://blog.innertune.com/letting-go-affirmations/

NHS. (2022, September 5). Thought Record CBT Exercise - Every Mind Matters. Nhs.uk. https://www.nhs.uk/every-mind-matters/mental-wellbeing-tips/self-help-cbt-techniques/thought-record/

Oldale, R. J. (2020, September 2). Psychology 101: The 12 Major Archetypes And Their Shadows. Master Mind Content. https://mastermindcontent.co.uk/psychology-101-the-12-major-archetypes-and-their-shadows/

Paperblanks Team. (2011, December 12). How To Make Collage-Art In A Journal: 5 Steps | Endpaper: The Paperblanks Blog. Paperblanks.com. https://blog.paperblanks.com/2011/12/how-to-create-a-collage-tips-from-featured-artist-virginia/

Pedersen , T. (2022, April 28). Triggers: What They Are, How They Form, and What to Do. Psych Central. https://psychcentral.com/lib/what-is-a-trigger#what-to-do-if-youre-triggered

Perry, C. (2015, August 12). The Jungian Shadow. Society of Analytical Psychology. https://www.thesap.org.uk/articles-on-jungian-psychology-2/about-analysis-and-therapy/the-shadow/

Perry, E. (2022, June 13). 8 Benefits of Shadow Work and How to Start Practicing It. Www.betterup.com. https://www.betterup.com/blog/shadow-work

Pickard, N. (2022, February 1). Self-Love and Self-Acceptance: 10 Affirmations. Rancho La Puerta. https://rancholapuerta.com/2022/02/01/self-love-and-self-acceptance-10-affirmations/

Psychology Today. (2020). Projection | Psychology Today. Psychology Today. https://www.psychologytoday.com/us/basics/projection

Ramirez, D. (n.d.). Triangle Breathing. https://positive.b-cdn.net/wp-content/uploads/Triangle-Breathing.pdf

Riddle, H. (n.d.). What Is the Shadow Archetype? Definition with Examples. Scribophile. https://www.scribophile.com/academy/what-is-the-shadow-archetype

Sara. (2022, February 4). 30 Affirmations for Emotional Healing - Spiritvibez. Spiritvibez. https://spiritvibez.com/affirmations-for-emotional-healing/

Says, J. (2024, January 31). Mindful Breathing. DBT. https://dialecticalbehaviortherapy.com/mindfulness/mindful-breathing/

Scott, E. (2024, February 12). What is body scan meditation? Verywell Mind. https://www.verywellmind.com/body-scan-meditation-why-and-how-3144782

Scotti, J. F. (2024, July 15). Why You Need to Get to Know Your Shadow Self. Psychology Today. https://www.psychologytoday.com/us/blog/buddhist-psychology-east-meets-west/202407/why-you-need-to-get-to-know-your-shadow-self

Seaver, M. (2023, March 29). 8 Mindfulness Breathing Exercises You Can Do Anywhere, Anytime. Real Simple. https://www.realsimple.com/health/mind-mood/breathing-exercises

Securly - Geolocation sharing. (2025). Damorementalhealth.com. https://damorementalhealth.com/understanding-shadow-work/#elementor-toc__heading-anchor-3

Shadow Work Affirmations. (n.d.). Theholisticpath.org. https://theholisticpath.org/shadow-work-affirmations/

Shafir, H. (2024, April 4). Trauma Release Exercises (TRE): Benefits, Types, & Getting Started. ChoosingTherapy.com. https://www.choosingtherapy.com/trauma-release-exercises/

Shketieva, R. (2025, February 20). 38 Powerful Affirmations for Emotional Healing. Affirmations.online. https://www.affirmations.online/38-powerful-affirmations-for-emotional-healing/#38_Powerful_Affirmations_for_Your_Emotional_Healing_Journey

Smookler, E. (2019, April 11). Beginner's body scan meditation. Mindful. https://www.mindful.org/beginners-body-scan-meditation/

Starting Therapy. (2024, October 31). What is Shadow Work Therapy? Access Therapy. https://www.accesstherapy.ca/speaking-with-my-therapist-blog/what-is-shadow-work-therapy

TalktoAngel . (2024, December 10). Is Suppressing Emotions Harmful? TalktoAngel. https://www.talktoangel.com/blog/is-suppressing-emotions-harmful

Task, A. (2024, July 18). Integrating Self and Shadow: A Journey to Embrace Wholeness. Allison Task. https://allisontask.com/integrating-the-self-and-shadow-self/

Telloian, C. (2021, October 4). Mindful Breathing: Benefits, Types, and How To. Psych Central. https://psychcentral.com/health/mindful-breathing#exercises-and-scripts

Tewari, A. (2022, August 5). 100+ Forgiveness Affirmations For Freedom, Healing & Peace. Gratitude - the Life Blog. https://blog.gratefulness.me/forgiveness-affirmations/

The Arbor Behavioral Healthcare. (2022, June 20). What Does it Mean to Suppress Emotions? The Arbor Behavioral Healthcare. https://thearbor.com/blog/what-does-it-mean-to-suppress-emotions/

Trauma Release Exercises (TRE) | Mindbody Toolkit. (n.d.). Osteopathy for All. https://osteopathyforall.co.uk/toolkits/mindbody-toolkit/trauma-release-exercises/

Turonova, S. (2024, April 22). 17 Healing Affirmations to Forgive Yourself. Silvia Turonova. https://silviaturon.com/17-healing-affirmations-to-forgive-yourself/

Uberboyo. (2018, August 28). Carl Jung's Active Imagination Technique. Medium. https://medium.com/@SteafanFox/carl-jungs-active-imagination-technique-2a622e00311

Villines, Z. (2023a, October 4). Repressed emotions: Symptoms, causes, and release. Www.medicalnewstoday.com. https://www.medicalnewstoday.com/articles/repressed-emotions#causes

Vinney, C. (2022, August 1). What Is a Projection Defense Mechanism? Verywell Mind. https://www.verywellmind.com/what-is-a-projection-defense-mechanism-5194898

Weaver, T. (2022, November 29). Embracing The Shadow - Carl Jung - Orion Philosophy. Orion Philosophy. https://orionphilosophy.com/the-shadow-carl-jung/

Wiginton, K. (2024, July 29). What Is Shadow Work? How to Start and Benefits. WebMD. https://www.webmd.com/mental-health/shadow-work#1-8

Young, M. (2023, February 3). Body Scan Meditation for Beginners: How and Why to Try It. Cleveland Clinic. https://health.clevelandclinic.org/body-scan-meditation

Zoharness. (2024, October 30). Shadow Work 02: The Shadow Archetypes - Zoharness - Medium. Medium. https://medium.com/@zoharness/shadow-work-02-the-shadow-archetypes-96716a955187

# Image Sources

1 Photo by James Wheeler: https://www.pexels.com/photo/silhouette-of-person-standing-on-bridge-414523/

2 Photo by Arina Krasnikova: https://www.pexels.com/photo/a-woman-in-knit-sweater-hugging-self-5709914/

3 Photo by Pixabay: https://www.pexels.com/photo/lonely-girl-sitting-on-a-doorway-236215/

4 Photo by Brett Sayles: https://www.pexels.com/photo/grayscale-photo-of-man-thinking-in-front-of-analog-wall-clock-1194196/

5 Photo by Andrea Piacquadio: https://www.pexels.com/photo/photo-of-woman-looking-at-the-mirror-774866/

6 Photo by Serkan Göktay: https://www.pexels.com/photo/woman-standing-near-body-of-water-66758/

7 Designed by Freepik. https://www.freepik.com/free-photo/classic-portrait-silhouette-man_31978821.htm

8 https://www.pexels.com/photo/broken-mirror-in-close-up-photography-10164349/

9 Janelle.teoh.19, CC BY-SA 4.0 <https://creativecommons.org/licenses/by-sa/4.0>, via Wikimedia Commons
https://commons.wikimedia.org/wiki/File:Diagram_of_Freud%27s_Psychoanalytic_Theory_of_Personality_.webp

10 Designed by Freepik. Source: https://www.freepik.com/free-photo/non-explicit-image-child-abuse_94965188.htm

11 Designed by Freepik. https://www.freepik.com/free-photo/terrifying-adult-silhouette-studio_60408270.htm

12 Designed by Freepik. https://www.freepik.com/free-photo/medium-shot-doctor-wearing-cape_8104154.htm

13 Photo by Alex Green: https://www.pexels.com/photo/black-couple-arguing-with-each-other-at-home-5699684/

14 Photo by Keira Burton: https://www.pexels.com/photo/man-and-woman-arguing-6147245/

15 Photo by Pixabay: https://www.pexels.com/photo/low-section-of-man-against-sky-247851/

16 Photo by Arina Krasnikova: https://www.pexels.com/photo/a-woman-in-knit-sweater-hugging-self-5709914/

17 https://www.pexels.com/photo/black-stackable-stone-decor-at-the-body-of-water-312839/

18 Photo by Julian Jagtenberg: https://www.pexels.com/photo/man-wearing-grey-shirt-standing-on-elevated-surface-103123/

19 Photo by Jess Bailey Designs: https://www.pexels.com/photo/gold-pen-on-journal-book-745760/